Peter Edwards

Candid Reasons for Renouncing the Principles of Anti-Paedobaptism

Also a short method with the Baptists

Peter Edwards

Candid Reasons for Renouncing the Principles of Anti-Paedobaptism
Also a short method with the Baptists

ISBN/EAN: 9783337312589

Printed in Europe, USA, Canada, Australia, Japan

Cover: Foto ©Lupo / pixelio.de

More available books at **www.hansebooks.com**

CANDID REASONS

FOR

RENOUNCING THE PRINCIPLES

OF

ANTI-PÆDOBAPTISM.

ALSO,

A SHORT METHOD WITH THE BAPTISTS.

BY

PETER EDWARDS,

SEVERAL YEARS PASTOR OF A BAPTIST CHURCH AT PORTSEA, HANTS

PHILADELPHIA:
PRESBYTERIAN BOARD OF PUBLICATION.
NO. 1334 CHESTNUT STREET.

CONTENTS.

	Page.
I. Introduction,—the Question stated,	7
II. Arguments of the Baptists against Infant Baptism,	15
III. Arguments in favour of Infant Baptism,	48
IV. A Scheme of the Controversy on Infant Baptism,	108
V. A Short Method with the Baptists,	133
VI. A Case submitted to the consideration of the Baptists,	180
VII. The Mode of Baptism; the Force of the Term, the Circumstances and Allusions considered,	181
VIII. The practical Use of Pædobaptism,	215

TO THE

CHURCH AND CONGREGATION

MEETING IN WHITES' ROW, PORTSEA, HANTS.

DEARLY BELOVED,

AFTER officiating among you, as Pastor and Minister, between ten and eleven years it seemed natural to address you in a publication intended to account for that change of sentiment in me, which has proved the occasion of our separation.

Two eminent writers, Mr. Booth and Dr. Williams, have both contributed to this. The latter has my acknowledgments; the former my animadversions. As Mr. Booth had no design to discover the fallacy of the Baptist scheme, I thought it proper to show in what way his book has operated, and is likely still to operate, contrary to the design of the author.

I have presented the whole scheme to the reader in the same point of view in which it was exhibited to my own mind. In composing it, I have endeavoured to avoid every thing foreign and bitter; that as the truth has been my object, I wished to say nothing that should divert the attention of the reader from it. Wishing that you and I may grow in grace and in the knowledge of Christ, I remain, in the same esteem and love,

Yours, in our common Lord,

PETER EDWARDS.

Portsea, January 12, 1795.

INTRODUCTION.

A FAIR STATEMENT OF THE INQUIRY.

THESIS I.

The only thing which, in any dispute, should engage our attention, is this: "What is truth?" And he who wishes to find it, will endeavour to adopt that plan which will bring him soonest to what he seeks. There are two things, in all matters of controversy, which greatly facilitate our search: First, that we set aside all those things about which we are agreed, and fix our attention to that only on which a difference of opinion may arise; and secondly, that this difference be stated in a manner the most plain and simple. To either of these, no person who seeks the truth can form the least objection.

THESIS II.

As this inquiry lies between those who pass under the denomination of Pædobaptists and Antipædobaptists, it will be proper, in order to ascertain wherein they differ on the subject of baptism, to give the sentiments of each. Antipædobaptists consider those persons as meet subjects of baptism, who are supposed to possess faith in Christ, and those only. Pædobaptists agree with them in this, that believers are proper subjects of baptism; but deny that such only are proper subjects. They think, that, together with such believing adults who have not yet been baptized, their infants have a right to baptism as well as their parents.

I have lately conversed with many Baptists, who knew so little of the sentiments of their brethren, that they supposed adult baptism was entirely rejected by Pædobaptists; and when I endeavoured, from their confessions of faith, &c. to convince my Baptist friends that they held adult baptism as well as themselves, some believed and marveled, but others remained in doubt.

THESIS III.

From this view of the sentiments of each, it appears that both parties are agreed on the article of adult baptism, which must therefore be set aside as a matter entirely out of dispute; for it can answer no good purpose for one to prove what the other will not deny. Now, seeing they are so far of one mind, (I speak of the subject, not of the mode,) the difference between them concerns infants only; and the simple question which remains to be decided, is this, Are infants fit subjects of baptism, or are they not? On this question the whole turns. The Pædobaptists affirm, and Antipædobaptists deny.

INTRODUCTION. 9

THESIS IV.

The simple question being as I have now stated it, Are infants fit subjects of baptism, or are they not? it will clearly follow, that all those places which relate to believers' baptism, can prove nothing on the side of Baptists; and the reason is, they have no relation to the question. To illustrate this, I ask a Baptist, Is an infant a fit subject of baptism? No, says he. Wherefore? Because the Scriptures say, Repent and be baptized—If thou believest, thou mayest—I interpose, and say, Your answer is not in point. I asked, Is an infant a fit subject of baptism? You answer by telling me that a penitent adult is such. But as I asked no question concerning an adult, the answer is nothing at all to the purpose. If I should ask whether an infant were a creature of the rational kind, would it be a good answer, if any person should say, that adults were of that description? No answer can be good, if it does not directly relate to the question proposed; for then, properly speaking, it is no answer to the question. And therefore, if I ask whether an infant is a proper subject of baptism, and another should bring twenty places to prove the propriety of baptizing adults; as all this would be nothing to the question, so nothing would be proved thereby, either for or against.

We may from hence estimate the strength

of each party, as they respect one another. The Pædobaptist has just so much strength against a Baptist, as his arguments weigh or the affirmative, and no more; and the Baptist has no more strength against him, but as his arguments weigh on the negative. Whatever arguments a Baptist may bring, to evince infant baptism to be wrong, whether they be many or few, good or bad, it is all his strength; he has not a grain more on his side. For as it lies on neither of these to prove adult baptism, (it being a thing professed and used by both, and therefore being no subject of dispute) those arguments that prove it, can have no place here. This being carefully observed, we shall see which of these has the fairest pretensions to truth.

THESIS V.

Whatever may, in reality, be the force of argument on either side, respecting this question, there can be no doubt but that side is the true one, on which the arguments are found to preponderate. If the arguments for infant baptism are stronger than any that can be produced against it, then infant baptism must be right; and so the easy and sure way of coming to a decision is, to collect the arguments on both sides, try their validity and compare them together. This, in the fear of God, I shall endeavour to do. First, I will set down the arguments against infant baptism, and examine them as I proceed;

and then those which make for it; and after that, I will compare them together in opposite columns. By this process, which is the fairest I am acquainted with, we shall see whether Baptists or Pædobaptists have the truth on their side.

The whole import of these propositions is—that both parties agree about adult baptism—that when a Baptist has proved adult baptism, he has proved nothing against a Pædobaptist—that the only question being this, Are infants fit subjects of baptism, or are they not? it is evident that those passages of Scripture, which prove adult baptism, will not answer this question—and, that arguments for and against being compared, that side is the true one, on which they preponderate.

If any thing can make this matter plainer, and I wish it to be made plain, perhaps the introduction of a short familiar dialogue may do it. We will therefore suppose a conversation between a Baptist and a Pædobaptist; the Baptist speaking as follows:

Bap. I wonder very much you should not agree with me in sentiment, respecting the subjects of baptism.

Pædo. There is nothing in this to wonder at, since we all see but in part: it is our happiness to believe to the saving of the soul.

Bap. That which makes me wonder is this, that the sentiment I hold is so clearly revealed in Scripture.

Pædo. What sentiment is that you hold

and which you say is so clearly revealed in Scripture?

Bap. I hold what is commonly called believers' baptism; or, that it is right to baptize a person professing faith in Christ.

Pædo. If that be your sentiment, I grant it is clearly revealed; but in this we are agreed, it is my sentiment as well as yours.

Bap. But this is not the whole of my sentiment. I meant to have said, that it is wrong to baptize infants.

Pædo. Then you and I differ only about infants?

Bap. If you grant adult baptism to be right, it is only about infants we differ.

Pædo. I do grant it. And then do you mean to say, that it is clearly revealed in Scripture, that it is wrong to baptize infants?

Bap. I do mean to say that.

Pædo. How do you prove it?

Bap. I prove it by Acts viii. 37. "If thou believest with all thine heart, thou mayest."

Pædo. You have indeed proved believers' baptism to be right; but I asked you, how you proved infant baptism to be wrong?

Bap. Must not infant baptism be wrong, if believers' baptism be right?

Pædo. No more than believers' baptism must be wrong, if infant baptism be right. Would you think I had proved that infants would be lost, by proving that believing adults would be saved?

Bap. Certainly I should not.

Pædo. Why?

Bap. Because the question would be only about infants; and we cannot infer the loss of an infant from the salvation of a believing adult.

Pædo. Very true. Then that which proves infant baptism wrong, must not be the same that proves adult baptism to be right.

Bap. I grant it, and think there is sufficient proof against it beside.

Pædo. This is the very point. You produce your proof against it, and I will produce mine for it. If your proof be found stronger against, than mine for, you have the truth on your side; if not, the truth is on mine.

Bap. Nothing can be more fair; and I am willing to put it to the test.

INFANT BAPTISM.

CHAPTER I.

ARGUMENTS AGAINST INFANT BAPTISM.

ARGUMENT I.

A person who has a right to a positive institution must be expressly mentioned as having that right; but infants are not so mentioned, therefore they have not that right.

As the whole force of this argument turns upon the words *express* and *explicit*, which Baptist writers commonly use, the reader, in order to form a just opinion upon the subject, should clearly understand their import. And since I shall often have occasion to use them, the reader will meet with an explanation of the term *explicit* in another place. At present it will be sufficient to say, that both these terms stand opposed to inference, analogy, and implication. And when the Baptists say there is no express command for infant baptism, they mean there is no command "in so many words," as "thou shalt baptize infants," or something equivalent. This being premised, I say of the argument, it is assuming, contracted, false. It is very assuming, because it seems to dictate to the ever-blessed God in what manner he ought to speak to his creatures. Since it is no where contained in his word, and he knows best how to communicate his mind to men, it little becomes such creatures as we are, to lay down rules by which he shall proceed. To such who thus assume, it may properly be said, " Who hath known the mind of the Lord? or who hath been his counsellor? For of him, and through him, and to him, are all things: to whom be glory for ever. Amen."

It is very contracted, because it supposes we cannot understand what God says, but when he speaks to us in one particular way. Certain it is that the most important things are set forth in Scripture, in many different ways; and we may come at the truth by an indirect, as certainly as by a direct expression: *e. g.* When the apostle says he was "caught up into the third heaven," I certainly know, there is a first and a second, though I no where had read expressly of any such thing. But what is most material, I affirm that

It is very false, because (to wave other instances, and fix on one only) a subject is admitted to a positive institution, and that admission is according to truth, and so held and practised by all, who use Christian rites; when yet there is no express law or example to support it, in all the word of God. It is the case of women, to which I allude, and their admission to the Lord's table.

I acknowledge it is right to admit them, and so do all, who use the Lord's Supper, but as to express law or example, there is no such thing in Scripture. If it be said, that women are fit subjects of baptism—that they are capable of religious advantages—that they have a right to church-membership, and therefore a right to the Lord's Supper, I grant it—And then the argument is false; for if women are admitted because they are fit subjects of baptism, &c. they are admitted by something, which is not express law or example. But the argument I am opposing says, "A person who has a right to positive institutions, must be expressly mentioned as having that right." Now, if women are not so mentioned with respect to the Supper, the practice of admitting them is wrong, or this argument is false. This argument indeed is false; the practice is by no means wrong. And to show the fallacy of the Baptist system at large, I will undertake, in the sequel, to prove that, upon the principles and reasonings of the Baptists, a woman, however qualified, can have no right whatever to the Lord's table.

"There is no express command or example for infant baptism!" This being a favourite argument with Baptists, and the case of women, in this respect, being the same as that of infants, they will not suffer an instance, so fatal to their system, to pass by without making an effort to overturn it. They know very well, I mean the thinking part, especially those who write, that they cannot maintain this argument against infants, without producing an explicit warrant for female communion. They therefore affirm, that the Scriptures afford such a warrant, and that it is found in 1 Cor. xi. 28. "Let a man [*Anthropos*] examine himself, and so let him eat of that bread, &c." It is certainly here, or nowhere. I have known many who took this for an express word for women. I did so myself for some years, till Mr. Booth's attempt to prove it convinced me of the contrary.

An express word, in the present case, must be one that specifies the sex; as Acts viii. 12, "they were baptized, both men and women." [*Andres kai gunaikes.*] But I ask, is *Anthropos* an express word for a woman? Mr. Booth affirms it is. Take it in his own words, vol. ii. p. 73. "In regard to the supposed want of an explicit warrant for admitting women to the holy table, we reply by demanding, does not Paul, when he says, Let a man examine himself, and so let him eat, enjoin a reception of the sacred Supper? Does not the term *Anthropos*, there used, often stand as a name of our species, without regard to sex? Have we not the authority of lexicographers, and, which is incomparably more, the sanction of common sense, for understanding it thus in that passage? When the sexes are distinguished and opposed, the word for a man is not *Anthropos*, but *Aneer*." This is all about the word, except a quotation, which is not material.

The reader is desired to observe, that, as Mr. B. has undertaken to produce an explicit warrant for female communion, he can derive no help from analogy, or inference, or any thing of that kind. The words he brings for proof must contain their own unequivocal evidence, independent of every other consideration. If this be not the case, his explicit warrant is a mere fiction.

Now for the explicit warrant. Mr. B. says, " Does not Paul, when he says, Let a man examine himself, and so let him eat, enjoin a reception of the sacred Supper? True. " Does not the term *Anthropos*, there used, often stand as the name of our species, without regard to sex?" True again. Observe this, OFTEN STAND! Not always. Does Mr. B. take this for an explicit warrant? What a demonstration! And how full to the point! But Mr. B. says it stands so in the text. How does he know it? Why he has two evidences of this; a lexicographer, *i. e.* a dictionary maker, and common sense. Common sense, he says, is the best of the two. However, I will take them together, and proceed to ask, How do they know that the term *Anthropos* stands in this text as a name of our species? They must know it either from the word itself, or from some other ground. That they cannot know it from the word itself, is evident by this single consideration, that a boy, who reads his Greek Testament, may meet with the word a hundred times, where the female sex can by no means be intended; nay, he may find it used several times, though Mr. B. could not, to distinguish the male from the female. Where then is its explicitness? He says it is often used as a name of our species. And is not our English word "man" used in the same way? Would Mr. B. take that to be an explicit word for a woman? If the word "man" be often used for a name of our species, as well as *Anthropos*, then one is just as explicit a word for a woman as the other; and so Mr. B. might as well have fixed on the English word for an explicit one, as the Greek. But had he done this, it would have ruined his book; and he has only escaped under the cover of a Greek term. If then, it cannot be known from the word itself, that females are intended, it matters not, in what other way we may know it, the Baptist argument is entirely ruined and lost.

But Mr. B. in the next sentence, will urge the matter further, and boldly affirm, that, "When the sexes are distinguished and opposed, the word for a man is not *Anthropos*, but *Aneer*." I know not what Mr. B. expected to prove by this assertion; for if it were true, I see not how it is to help him in respect to his explicit warrant; but as it is false, it cannot help him in any form, except it be to make him more cautious in future. This assertion, if it proceeded from ignorance, is, in a reader and writer like Mr. B. far too bad; if it did not proceed from ignorance, it is far worse. I am willing to suppose the former, and acquit him of the latter.

Against this assertion of Mr. B. I will now place nineteen instances; in every one of which there is a distinction and opposition of the sexes, and the word for a man is not *Aneer*, but *Anthropos*. Some of these are in the Septuagint, and others in the New Testament. Gen. ii. 24, "Therefore shall a man [*Anthropos*] leave his father and his mother, and cleave unto his wife." Gen. xxvi. 11. "And Abimelech charged all his people, saying, He that toucheth this man [*Anthropou*] or his wife, shall surely be put to death." Gen. xxxiv. 14. "And Simeon and Levi, the brethren of Dinah, said, We cannot do this thing, to give our SISTER to one [*Anthropo*] that is uncircumcised." Deut. xx. 7, "And what man [*Anthropos*] is there that hath betrothed a wife, and hath not taken her?" Deut. xvii. 5. "Then shalt thou bring forth that man, [*Anthropon*] or that WOMAN." Jer. xliv. 7. "Wherefore commit ye this great evil against your souls, to cut off from you man [*Anthropon*] and WOMAN, child and suckling?" For other instances in the Septuagint see Gen. ii. 18; Lev. xix. 20; Num. xxv. 8; Deut. xxi. 15—xxii. 30; Esther iv. 11.

Matt. xix. 10. "His disciples say unto him, If the case of the man [*Anthropou*] be so with his WIFE, it is not good to marry." Matt. xix. 3. "The Pharisees also came unto him, tempting him, and saying unto him, Is it lawful for a man [*Anthropo*] to put away his WIFE for every cause?" Mark x. 7. "For this cause shall a man [*Anthropos*] leave his father and mother, and cleave to his wife." 1 Cor. vii. 1. "Now concerning the things whereof ye wrote unto me, it is good for a man [*Anthropo*] not to touch a woman." Matt. xix. 5. "For this cause shall a man [*Anthropos*] leave his father and mother, and cleave to his *wife*." Rev. ix. 7, 8. "And their faces were as the faces of men [*Anthropón;*] and they had hair as the hair of *women*." Eph. v. 31. "For this cause shall a man [*Anthropos*] leave his father and mother, and shall be joined unto his *wife*."

After I had collected some of these instances, which I have here set down, I mentioned the sentence of Mr. B. and likewise the instances which lay against it, to a Baptist minister, who happened to be at my house. He thereupon took the Greek Testament, and read those places to which I directed him. When he had done this, he was greatly surprised at the incautiousness of Mr. B. and at the same time, made the best apology for him, which the case would admit of. I then observed, that, had Mr. B. affirmed that *Aneer* was more commonly used to distinguish the sexes, than *Anthropos*, he would have been right. Yes, said he, but that would not have answered Mr. B.'s purpose. Which indeed was very true; for he, having all through his book insisted that in fants should not be baptized, because there was no express warrant for it, was compelled, by his own reasoning, to bring forward an explict warrant for female communion. And when he comes to prove that there is such a warrant in Scripture for female right to the Lord's Supper, he first of all falls upon presumptive proof, " Does not the term *Anthropos* often stand as a name of our species?" As if he had said, If this word often stands as a name of our species, I presume it is possible it may so stand in this text. In the next place he falls upon inferential proof, and sets a lexicographer and common sense to infer (for they could do no other) that so it must mean in the text. And lastly, to make it still worse, he makes an evident mistake, when he says, that, when the sexes are distinguished and opposed, the word for a man is not *Anthropos*, but *Aneer*. This is all Mr. B. is pleased to give the reader, instead of an explicit warrant—presumption, inference, and mistake; and if either he, or any of his readers, can satisfy themselves with such an explicit warrant as this, they can neither of them be esteemed very nice in this article.

But, to set Mr. B. and his explicit warrant in a clear point of light, the reader has only to contemplate those two facts which have just passed under his eye; namely, that *Anthropos* is often used as a name of our species, as Mr. B. affirms; and likewise that it is often used to distinguish one sex from the other. Now with these two facts in view [*viz. An-*

thropos is often used as a name of our species, and often it is not so used,] if a question be started concerning its meaning in any text, let it be 1 Cor. xi. 28, the reader will see at once that it is no explicit word, because he will stand in need of a third thing, to determine in what sense it is used there; whereas, if the word were explicit, nothing else would be necessary to fix the sense. Now as the facts weigh on both sides, OFTEN against OFTEN, and as the reader wants a third thing to settle the import of the word in this text, I ask, what is this third thing? Lexicographers and common sense, says Mr. B. Nay, no ambiguity, sir, we are now talking of explicitness Why did you not say, analogy and inference? Shocking! What! give up the cause at once! But what, I say again, is this third thing? Is Mr. B. afraid of telling? I wish, however, he would write again, and say in plain terms what it is. Is it what you speak of in the latter part of the defence, *viz.* " that women have the same pre-requisites as men, and that male and female are one in Christ?" Very good.—Proceed.—Therefore —I say, go on, do not be afraid, this will bring you safe to your conclusion; for it is only analogy and inference. Inference and analogy! and upon a positive institution too! I cannot bear the terms; I would much rather call them lexicographers and common sense; for were I to call them inference and analogy, it would ruin my whole book. It is very true, Mr. B.; but at the same time, is it not better your book should be ruined by plain dealing, than that your reputation should seem to be stained by acting an artful part? But after all, here is a third thing wanting to settle the meaning of this ambiguous word. And what does it signify by what name we call this third thing? For whether we name it analogy, or inference, or lexicographer, or common sense (which two last are Mr. B.'s names, as he could not bear the others on a positive institution,) it comes still to the same thing; it shows that this is no explicit word for females, and consequently, as there is no other, this argument is ruined.

What I have now animadverted upon is all Mr. B. says, that can even pretend to evince an explicit warrant. But since the whole of it, upon his principles, is as curious a defence of female right to the Lord's table as ever was presented to the public, I will pay him the compliment of surveying it, and taking it to pieces, in due time and place. In the mean time I do not blame Mr. B. for not being able to produce an explicit warrant for women; it is what no man is able to do; but I do blame him for using such reasoning as he has done, and then passing it upon the public under the colour of explicit proof.

It is a common opinion that Baptists and Pædobaptists do reason differently on positive institutions; that the former invariably insist upon express proof, while the latter admit the force of inferential reasoning. It is true they profess to reason differently, and they actually do sometimes; but then it is only according to the mood they may be in, and the matter they may have in hand. Let the matter of debate be a little varied, and they reason on positive institutions precisely in the same way.

I have taken the liberty in time past, to ask Pædobaptists why they baptized their infants? One has told me, that infants were circumcised, and therefore should now be baptized; inferring their baptism from circumcision. Another has told me, that our Lord took infants into his arms, and blessed them, and said they were of the kingdom of heaven; so inferring their baptism from the language and conduct of Christ. At hearing this, the Baptists smile, and think it very foolish reasoning.

I have also taken the liberty to ask Baptists, why they admitted women to the Lord's table? One informed me that women were partakers of the grace of God; inferring their right to communicate from their grace. Another told me, that women had been baptized; and inferred their right to the supper from their baptism. A third gave me to understand, that women did eat of the paschal lamb, and from thence inferred their right to the Lord's table. A fourth told me that women were creatures of God as well as men; and so inferred their right from their creation. These Baptists did all infer, and, as Mr. B. says of Pædobaptists, not feeling the ground on which they stood, they agreed in one conclusion, but did not agree in the premises from which it should be drawn.

It may perhaps be said, that these persons did not possess logical exactness; that they were not aware of the impropriety of demanding plain, express, unequivocal proof; and then, as it suited their convenience, flying directly to inference, implication, and analogy; and that too on a positive ordinance. I grant they were plain persons, and did not see the inconsistency of this conduct. Well, we will betake ourselves to men of skill, to those who are acquainted with logical precision; and then let us see how they act in this business. What think you of Mr. Booth, as a man of erudition and logical attainment? Does Mr. B., say you, employ inferential reasoning on a positive institution? Nothing in the world more certain. What! Mr. B.; he who has written so many hundred pages with a view to expose it? Yes, that identical Mr. B. to the reproach of all consistency, does, in that very work, when sad necessity compels, even deal in this same inferential reasoning. I will not evidence this now, since I have promised to notice his whole defence of women in a more proper place.

All I am concerned to do in this place, is to show that this argument of the Baptists is false. The argument is this: " A person who has a right to a positive institution, must be expressly mentioned as having that right·

but infants are not so mentioned, &c." Tha the argument is false, appears from these facts:

I. The scriptures do not countenance it. For as it is not proved by any part of the word of God, being neither set down in the words, nor yet in the sense of holy writ, and therefore a fiction, invented by men to support a particular opinion; so it stands directly against God's holy word. And this is evident from hence; that though women are expressly said to have been baptized, they are never said to have received the Lord's supper. The Scriptures, therefore, in plain opposition to this false argument, leave us to conclude their right to the Lord's supper from their baptism, together with other grounds. Thus it has no support from Scripture.

II. The Baptists themselves do not countenance it; for though they have written whole books on the strength of it, they are compelled to desert it, and do desert it, the moment the subject is varied. For after they have vapoured ever so long, and ever so loud, about "no express law—no explicit warrant for infant baptism—infant baptism is no where mentioned in Scripture;" let any one put it upon them to prove the right of women to the supper, and I will answer for it he will hear no more of express law on that head. He will find that all this hollow sound which signifies nothing, will die away, and each will shift for himself the best way he can, and fly for aid to analogy and inference. Women, say they, may be gracious — Women were baptized — Women did eat of the paschal lamb — Women are creatures of God, as well as men and therefore — Therefore what? Why therefore they should receive the Lord's supper. What now has become of their express law? It is deserted, completely deserted; nor will they adopt it again till infant baptism is resumed. The Baptists, therefore, do not countenance it.

III. Mr. Booth himself does not countenance it; I mean, not always countenance it. For though he has demanded explicit proof for infant baptism, and has contended that if such proof cannot be adduced, the baptism of infants must be wrong, yet, when he comes to produce an explicit warrant for female communion, he is content, nay, stop, I cannot say he is content, but he is compelled to fly to presuming, to implication, to analogy, to inference, to make out an explicit warrant! All this we engage to prove, and to make a proper use of it in the sequel. And I cannot help observing, that if female communion cannot be supported on the principle of this argument, how idle a thing it is to forge a rule to operate against infants only.

Finally, as this argument militates against female communion, as well as infant baptism, they must either both be wrong, or the argument itself must be false. That the argument is false, is sufficiently evident, as it not only has no support from Scripture, but lies directly against it; and from what I have observed, in many recent conversations, I do not suppose there is a single Baptist in the kingdom that will even dare to stick to it. For after they had urged this argument upon me, I have turned the question from infant baptism to female communion, and I do not recollect one, either minister or private person, but has, in little more than a quarter of an hour, entirely given up the argument. And if Mr. B. should think proper to take up his pen once more on this subject, I have not a doubt but I should be able to compel even him, as well as many of his brethren, to relinquish it as a false argument; and I hope he will take up his pen once again, and vindicate his defence of female communion.

I have been the longer on this argument, because as it is very frequently urged, so it contains precisely one half of the Baptist strength. This argument, therefore, being destroyed, just half their strength is gone And if any one should be inclined to cry out, "There is no explicit example—there is no express law for infant baptism," &c. any person has it in his power to quiet him almost in an instant, should he only ask him to produce his explicit law, for female communion. Thus much for this bad argument; and I pass to the other.

ARGUMENT II.

The Scriptures require faith and repentance as requisite to baptism; but as infants cannot have these, they are not proper subjects of baptism. Infants, say the Baptists cannot believe, cannot repent; and none should be baptized without faith, &c.

THE most expeditious way of destroying this argument, would be this. They say the Scriptures require faith and repentance in order to baptism. I ask, Of whom? The answer must be, Of adults; for the Scriptures never require them of infants, in order to any thing. Then frame the argument thus:—The Scriptures require faith and repentance of ADULTS, in order to baptism. Now you see infants are gone, they have nothing to do with the argument; or if they must be brought in, the argument will run thus:—The Scriptures require faith and repentance of ADULTS, in order to baptism; but as INFANTS cannot have these, they are unfit subjects of that ordinance. Now it is a glaring sophism; with adults in one proposition, and infants in the other. Were I only to leave the argument thus, and say no more upon it, it would not be possible to save it from destruction; but since it is the only remaining half of the Baptist strength, I will examine it more at large.

In order to judge of the real worth of an argument, I lay down this rule : " Every argument that will prove against an evident truth ; or, which is the same thing, every argument which will support a falsehood, is clearly a bad argument." This rule is self-evident; for that must needs be false, which tends to prove a falsehood.

I will proceed by this rule, and attempt to show, I. That this argument is entirely fallacious. II. Point out wherein its fallacy consists.

I. Of the fallacy of this argument. The principle of it is, that infants are excluded from baptism, because something is said of baptism which will not agree to infants. To see therefore the tendency of this argument, whether it will prove on the side of truth or error, I will try its operation on these four subjects.

1. On the circumcision of infants. That infants were circumcised, is a fact. That they were circumcised by the express command of God, is a proof of right. They were actually circumcised, and it was right they should be so. Therefore, that they were proper subjects of that institution, is an evident truth. Now on this truth I mean to try the argument, to see if it will prove for or against it.

Circumcision, as it was a solemn entering into the church of God, did fix an obligation on the circumcised, to conform to the laws and ordinances of that church. Hence that speech, Acts xv. 24. "Ye must be circumcised, and keep the law;" which would have been just, if circumcision had not been abolished. The apostle says, Gal. v. 3. "Every man who is circumcised, is a debtor to do the whole law." His meaning is, if circumcision be in force, so must its obligation too. And Rom. ii. 25, he says, "Circumcision profiteth, if thou keep the law; but, if thou be a breaker of the law, thy circumcision is made uncircumcision." The sum of this is, he that was circumcised became a debtor; if he kept the law to which he was bound, his circumcision would profit; but if he violated it, his circumcision became a nullity.

Now I ask, Did it agree to an infant to become a debtor? Did it agree to an infant to break or keep the law? Mr. Booth shall answer both. To the first he says, vol. ii. page 151, "Infants are not capable of contracting either with God or man;—that, to suppose any such thing, insults the understanding and feelings of mankind. For, as Bishop Sanderson observes, In personal obligations no man is bound without his own consent." To the others he answers, "The minds of mere infants are not capable of comparing their own conduct with the rule of duty: they have, properly speaking, no conscience at all." Infants therefore could not become debtors; they could not keep the law. Very well. Then it is clear there was something said of circumcision, which did no more agree to infants, than if it had been said, Repent, and be baptized.

In this respect, baptism and circumcision are upon a level; for there is something said concerning both, which will by no means agree to infants. Infants, on the one hand, can neither believe nor repent; and these are connected with baptism; and, on the other hand, infants cannot become debtors, they cannot keep the law; and these are connected with circumcision. And then if we say, as the Baptists do, that infants, since they cannot believe or repent, must not be baptized, because faith and repentance are connected with baptism; we must say likewise, infants cannot become debtors, they cannot keep the law; and because these are connected with circumcision, they must not be circumcised. And then it follows, that this argument, by proving against a known truth, appears a fallacious argument.

But it may be said, circumcision of infants was commanded of God, and was therefore certainly right. To this I answer, that that is the very principle on which I proceed, and it is that very thing which proves fatal to this argument; for the circumcision of infants being an evident truth, and the argument before us proving against it, it is a plain demonstration of its absurdity and fallacy. Now if this argument be such, that had it been used by a Jew in the land of Canaan, it would have proved against an ordinance of God, I would fain know, if its nature can in any measure be changed, merely on its being used by a Baptist, and in a different climate? I proceed to try it,

2. On the baptism of Jesus Christ. The baptism of Christ is a known fact; and that he was a fit subject, is an acknowledged truth. It is likewise certain, that, as he was no sin-

ner, he could have no repentance; and since he needed no salvation from sin, he could not have the faith of God's elect; that is, he could not have that faith which the Scriptures require for baptism.

Now the tendency of this argument being to prove, that those who cannot have faith and repentance are unfit subjects of baptism; and Scripture informing us that our Lord Jesus was baptised, who could have neither, the dilemma therefore will be this; either the baptism of Christ was wrong, or else this argument is false. It is impossible to suppose the first, that the baptism of Christ was wrong; we must therefore affirm the last, that this argument is false: because that argument must be false which proves against an evident truth.

Again, when it is said in the argument, that the Scriptures require faith and repentance, in order to baptism; I ask, Do they require them of all, or of some only? If it be said, they are required of all; then, as before noted, it proves against the baptism of Jesus Christ. If it be said, they require them of some only; then the argument has no force: for, in that case, it would run thus—Faith and repentance are required only of some, in order to baptism; and now the consequence will be, that some may be baptized without them. And nothing would remain then, but that it be determined, who should be baptized without faith, and who with.

View it which way we will, the argument

is miserably bad. The Baptists, however, in this case, fly to its relief by saying, "that Jesus Christ, on account of the dignity of his person, was exempted from this rule." How this will mend the matter, I see not; for now it is acknowledged to be a rule which will admit of exception. And then I have only to ask, How many exceptions does it admit, and what are they? Neither would it be better to say, that Christ was baptized, to set us an example. For then we should have an example of one, who, being incapable of faith and repentance, was baptized without them. And in this view, his example will weigh in favour of infant baptism. I will try it again,

3. On the salvation of infants. That infants may be the subjects of salvation is universally admitted; that those, who die in infancy, are actually glorified, is also granted; and yet there is something said concerning salvation, which will by no means agree to infants—" He that believeth shall be saved; he that believeth not shall be damned," &c.

What shall we say in this case? Why, the same as before. If infants must not be baptized, because something is said of baptism, which does not agree to infants; then, by the same rule, infants must not be saved, because something is said of salvation, which does not agree to infants. And then, the same consequence again follows, that this argument, by proving against an acknowledged truth, proves itself to be fallacious.

And now, since it falls in with my present design, and may serve to relieve and inform the reader, I will present him with two specimens of reasoning on the same text; one of which concludes against infant baptism, and the other for it. The reader may adopt that which pleases him best.

The first specimen shall be that of Mr. B. vol. ii. page 309, where he adopts the remark of Mr. Chambers: "What they [the German Baptists] chiefly supported their great doctrine on, was those words of our Saviour: 'He that believeth, and is baptized, shall be saved.' As none but adults are capable of believing, they argued, 'that no others are capable of baptism.'" If these had gone one step further, their argument would have been lost: *e. g.* As none but adults are capable of believing, none but adults are capable of being saved. This with the Baptists is a favourite text; and they argue upon it from the order of the words. If, say they, faith goes before baptism; then infants must not be baptized, because they have no faith.

The other is that of Dr. Walker, out of his Modest Plea, page 179. His words are these: "If none must be baptized but he that believes, because believing is set first; then none must be saved but he that is baptized, because baptizing is set first. And then, what better argument can be made for infant baptism? They must be baptized if we will have them saved; because they cannot be saved without being baptized; for baptizing goes before saving. And yet from the same text, and by the same way of arguing, it may be proved, that no infants are saved, but those that believe; because believing is set before saving. And not only so, but whereas it is not said, he that believeth not shall not be baptized; it is said, he that believeth not shall be damned."

The difference between the reasoning of these two, lies in this: The Baptists reason on a part of the text only, and the Doctor reasoned on the whole. And to show how miserably fallacious the reasoning of the Baptists is, I will lay down a plan of their logic on this text, which will produce more conclusions than there are principal words in that part of the verse. The place is Mark xvi. 16. " He that believeth and is baptized, shall be saved." Now as the Baptists reason from the order of the words, I will mark them with figures, ^{1}believeth—^{2}baptized—^{3}saved.

The logic is as follows: Take the first and second, believeth—baptized—and say with the Baptists—

1. None are to be baptized but such as believe, because believing must be before baptizing.—" ^{1}Believeth"—" ^{2}Baptized."

This will conclude against infant baptism.

Next take the first and third—believeth—saved—and say in the same way:

2. None are to be saved, but such as believe, because believing must be before saving.—" ^{1}Believeth"—" ^{3}saved."

This concludes against infant salvation.

Now take the second and third—baptized—saved—and argue in the same manner:

3. None are to be saved, but such as are baptized, because baptizing must go before saving.—" ²Baptized"—" ³saved."

This will conclude on the side of infant baptism, they must be baptized, or they cannot be saved. As Dr. Walker reasons.

Lastly, take all three—believeth—baptized—saved—and say:

4. None are to be saved but such as believe and are baptized, because believing and baptizing must be before saving—" ¹Believeth"—" ²baptized"—" ³saved."

This concludes against the salvation of believers in Jesus Christ, if they have not been baptized. And so upon the principle of the Baptists, it concludes against the salvation of all Pœdobaptists.

All these conclusions, arising from the same way of reasoning, may serve as a specimen to show the fallacious mode of arguing against infant baptism, adopted by the Baptists.

Let it be tried once more,

5. On the temporal subsistence of infants. As the reader may perceive the drift of the reasoning, on these instances, I will use but few words on the present one. Now that infants should be supported, not only Scripture, but nature itself teaches. And yet, if we form the Baptist argument, on a few places of Scripture, it may be proved, in opposition

to Nature and Scripture both, that infants should actually be left to starve.

We have nothing to do but mention the texts, and apply their reasoning to them. Isaiah i. 19. "If ye be willing and obedient, ye shall eat the good of the land." 2 Thess. iii. 10. "If any would not work, neither should he eat." Take the first, and say with the Baptist in another case: Willingness and obedience are required of those who are to eat the good of the land; but since infants can neither will nor obey, they must not eat the good of the land. In the same way let the other be taken: He that will not work, neither shall he eat; infants cannot will to work, then infants must not eat.

This argument, in whatever way it is viewed, proves against the truth. Is it a truth, that infants should subsist? This argument proves against it. Is it a truth, that infants may be saved? This argument will prove the contrary. Was Christ rightly baptized? According to this argument it could not be. Were infants proper subjects of circumcision? This argument will prove they were not. Then, if it invariably support a falsehood, we are compelled to say it is a false argument.

II. I will point out wherein this fallacy consists. As this argument, notwithstanding it is false, is used by the Baptists in general, both learned and unlearned, I will attempt to lay open its fallacy; and thereby put those persons upon their guard, who may be in danger of being seduced by it. The judicious reader may have observed, that I slightly hinted at the outset, wherein its fault consisted; but to make it yet more evident what that fault is, of which it is guilty, I will take the liberty of saying a few words more.

That particular rule, against which this argument offends, is this: "*Non debet plus esse in conclusione quam erat in præmissis. Ratio manifesta est, quia conclusio educenda est ex præmissis.*" That is, "There should not be more in the conclusion than was in the premises. The reason is plain, because the conclusion is to be drawn from the premises." We will try to make this plain, by examples both of true and false reasoning.

1. In the Baptist way of reasoning. When the Scriptures say, "Repent and be baptized;" and, "If thou believest thou mayest," &c. they address only sinful adults; and then, an argument formed upon them should reach no further than adults of the same description. But the Baptists form their fallacious argument on these passages, by bringing infants into the conclusion, who, as they are not addressed, are not at all concerned in the premises. This will appear plain by three instances on the Baptist plan.

The Baptist argument runs thus: The Scriptures require faith and repentance in order to baptism; but infants have not faith and repentance: therefore they are not to be baptized. Now as the Scriptures require faith and repentance only of adults, we must place that word in the argument, and then it will stand in this form: The Scriptures require faith and repentance of ADULTS in order to baptism; but INFANTS cannot have these: therefore infants are not fit subjects of baptism. In the same way, we may form the two following instances, *viz.* The Scriptures require faith and repentance of adults in order to salvation; but infants cannot have these: therefore infants cannot be saved. Again, He [an adult] who will not work, neither should he eat; but an infant cannot will to work, therefore an infant should not eat. The reader may perceive, that by placing the word adults in one proposition, and infants in the other, (which makes it a sophism,) there are three things proved in the same way, *viz.* That infants cannot be saved—that infants should not eat—that infants should not be baptized. And so, for the same reason, that an infant cannot be saved, that an infant should not eat, it will follow, that an infant should not be baptized. For all these are equally true, and supported by the same reasoning. And it is in the same way, that this argument proves against the baptism of Christ, and the circumcision of infants. We will now view these three instances,

2. In the Pædobaptist way of reasoning. We will place the same word in each proposition, thus: The Scriptures require faith and repentance of adults in order to baptism; but some adults have no faith, no repentance; therefore some adults are not to be baptized. Again, The Scriptures require faith and re-

pentance of adults in order to salvation; but some adults do not believe nor repent; therefore some adults will not be saved. Once more—He [an adult] who will not work, neither should he eat; but some adults will not work; therefore some adults should not eat. Now by placing the word adult in each proposition, without which it would be a sophistical argument, the reader may see, that as infants can have no place in either, there is nothing to forbid their support, their salvation, or their baptism. They only prove that an idle adult should not be supported; that an impenitent adult will not be saved; and, that he has no right at all to baptism.

Once more—As I have nothing in view, so much as truth, I have a great desire to make this matter plain to the meanest capacity. For if I am clearly understood in this part, my end on the present argument is attained; and what I have before advanced upon it will be, in a great measure, useless. The reader, therefore, is desired to observe, that the design of this argument is to conclude against the baptism of infants. Then, as infants are to be in the conclusion, they must also be in the premises; for the rule says, "there should not be more in the conclusion than was in the premises; because the conclusion is to be drawn from the premises."

Now to make the argument of the Baptists consistent with itself, we must place infants in the premises as well as in the conclusion; and then the argument will stand thus: The

Scriptures require faith and repentance of infants in order to baptism; but infants have not faith, &c.; therefore infants are not to be baptized. The reader may discern an agreement, in the parts of the argument, with each other; it has infants in each part, as well in the premises, as in the conclusion. But then, the fallacy of it is more strikingly evident than before: for the error, which before crept into the middle, does here stand in front; it is in this proposition, the Scriptures require faith and repentance of infants in order to baptism, which is not true; for infants are never required to repent or believe, in order either to baptism or salvation. Whereas before, when it was said the Scriptures require faith and repentance of adults in order to baptism; but infants have not faith, &c., the error consisted in putting in the word "infants," who have no concern at all in the requirement.

By placing one thing in the premises, and another in the conclusion, which is done by the Baptists, in this argument, we may be able to evince any absurdity, however glaring. This being the manner of the Baptist argument, nothing more is necessary to take off its force against infants, but to make the premises and conclusion to correspond with each other. That is, while it continues to be a sophism, it proves against infants; but it ceases to prove against them, as soon as it is made a good argument. *e. g.* Faith and repentance are required of adults in order to baptism; but infants have not these: therefore infants are not to be baptized. This is nothing more than a pure sophism, and, as such, it concludes against infants; but all its force against infants is set aside by making it good, thus: Faith and repentance are required in adults in order to baptism; but some adults have not faith and repentance: therefore some adults are not to be baptized. The reader may see, that now it is a fair argument, all its force against infants is gone.

Having said thus much on the fallacy of this argument, I shall only add one specimen of its mode of operation; and that is a specimen, in which it will conclude two contrary ways, on one place of Scripture, Rom. ii. 25, " For circumcision verily profiteth, if thou keep the law; but if thou be a breaker of the law, thy circumcision is made uncircumcision."

Now the Baptist argument, on the first member of this text, will operate thus: Circumcision verily profiteth, if thou keep the law; but infants could not keep the law: therefore their circumcision must be unprofitable, that is, is no circumcision, a mere nullity; and this reflects on the wisdom of God. But if we form the same argument on the other member, it will be no nullity neither, for thus it will run: If thou be a breaker of the law, thy circumcision is made uncircumcision: But infants could not break the law; therefore their circumcision could not be made uncircumcision, $i.\,e.$ a nullity. Such is this Baptist argument, that it will prove infant circumcision to be something or nothing, according to that part of the text on which it is formed; and it is therefore evidently no more than a sophism.

I have endeavoured to make the reader see, not only that this argument is false, but wherein that fallacy consists. That it is false, appears in this, that in every instance it opposes a known truth; it opposes the circumcision of infants—the baptism of Jesus Christ—the salvation of infants—and, their temporal subsistence. The nature of the fallacy is the placing of adults in the premises, and infants in the conclusion; which any person, who has the least knowledge of the art of reasoning, must see instantly to be repugnant to the laws of truth. If the method I have taken to show wherein the fault consists, should not be familiar to any reader, it is possible he may not apprehend me; if so, I would advise him to read it repeatedly, and with serious attention; for I am not without hope, that even the most common capacity, with due attention, will clearly comprehend my meaning. On the other hand, I have no doubt, but many will readily enter into the method, and see what a fallacious argument is made use of to support an opinion, I am compelled to desert.

These two arguments being taken away, a Baptist has nothing left to place against infant baptism. I have not met with a single person, who, when desired to produce the strongest arguments against infants, could advance any thing more than what is contained in these two. While I thought it right to oppose the baptism of infants, I made use of them against it; but when they appeared, as they really are, very erroneous and bad, I gave them up; and from that time have never been able to preach a baptizing sermon. I saw that the whole strength of a Baptist was gone.

By the removal of these two arguments, thus much is gained; that whatever can be advanced, on the part of infants, will stand with undiminished force. For it will now avail nothing to say, with the first argument, there is no express law for infant baptism; nor will it be of any use to affirm, according to the second, that infants have no faith, no repentance; because the arguments themselves being fallacious, whatever may be urged from them, will be entirely devoid of force against infant baptism.

Having now finished what I intended on the arguments, on one side, I proceed to those on the other. I am well persuaded, that the Scriptures cannot favour both sides; and had the arguments against infant baptism been good, I am convinced that nothing in the word of God would have given it any countenance. But since the truth must be either for or against the baptism of infants, and the arguments against being futile, it is certain the truth must lie on the other side.

CHAPTER II.

Arguments on the side of Infant Baptism.

Infant baptism is to be proved, in the same way, as female communion. In the case of female communion, all the Baptists I have ever conversed with, on that subject, make use of inference and analogy; and, though in them it is ridiculous, they are not able to prove it in any other way. And this method is even adopted by Mr. Booth, as I shall more plainly evince in another place; though glaringly inconsistent with his own principles.

As I am now to advance proof in favour of infant baptism, the simple method I mean to adopt will be the following. In the first place, it is a fact acknowledged by the Baptists themselves, that infants were at an early period constituted members of the church of God. In the next place, I shall produce proof, that they have a right to be so now; and that the constitution of God by which they were made members, has not been altered to this day. In the last place, I shall lay down this dilemma, which will conclude the whole business, namely: As infants by a divine and unaltered constitution have a right to be received as church members, they must be received either with baptism or without it. If they are not to be received without baptism, then, the consequence is, that they must be baptized, because they must be received.—I now request the reader's attention to each of these in their order.

ARGUMENT I.

God has constituted in his Church the membership of infants, and admitted them to it by a religious rite.

In this argument it is proper to take notice of two parts.

I. The church-membership of infants.—A church is a society that stands in special relation to God, being instituted for religious purposes. When the persons composing this society appear openly in such relation to God, it is called a visible church; and of such an one I now speak. The relation between God and this society, is formed by God himself, by declaring he is, and will be their God. This declaration of God which constituted that relation, which indeed did exist from the beginning, had an equal regard to adults and infants; " I will be a God unto thee, and to thy seed after thee." And hence both young and old, who had been duly entered, were considered as children of the covenant and the kingdom, that is, of the church. The rite of circumcision being performed, the circumcised was presented to the Lord; which is a mode of expression to signify a public entering into church-fellowship.

The case, as now stated, is, I suppose, commonly admitted. It is granted by Baptists, who are the most likely of any to deny it, that infants were members of the Jewish church. Mr. Booth grants it, vol. ii. 224. So does Mr. Keach, Gold Refined, page 113. "That children were admitted members of the Jewish church is granted." And indeed it is not possible to deny this, without denying that adults themselves were members, which would be the same as denying that God had a church in the world. Infants, therefore, were constituted by God himself, members of his own visible church.

II. Infants, in order to visible membership, were the subjects of a religious rite. That circumcision was a religious rite, is as easily proved, as that baptism and the Lord's supper are such. Mr. Booth, in this case, is in a strait betwixt two; he is not willing flatly to deny it, nor yet can he prevail on himself to acknowledge it. He is very tender upon the subject, as if he saw some formidable consequence lurking beneath it. See what he says, vol. ii. 250. "Baptism is an appointment purely religious, and intended for purposes entirely spiritual; but circumcision, besides the spiritual instruction suggested by it, was a sign of carnal descent, a mark of national distinction, and a token of interest in those temporal blessings that were promised to Abraham." Now can any living soul tell from whence Mr. Booth had all this? Was it from the Koran or Talmud? To show he never took his notion from the Bible, I will set the Bible against him, and him against it.

Booth.	*Bible.*
It was a token of interest in temporal blessings.	It was a token of the covenant between God and Abraham, to be a God to him and his seed.
It was a sign of carnal descent.	It was a sign of circumcision, *i. e.* of the heart and spirit.
It was a mark of national distinction.	It was a seal of the righteousness of faith.

Now compare Mr. Booth with fact.

Booth.	*Fact*
It was a token of interest in temporal blessings.	Many had the interest without the token, and many had the token without the interest.
It was a mark of national distinction.	Many other nations had the same mark. So it was a distinction which did not distinguish.
It was a sign of carnal descent.	All Abraham's male servants, and many proselytes, were circumcised. Either these were descended from Abraham, or Mr. Booth's sign was deceptive.

See what the love of hypothesis can do! Could any man have given a poorer account of circumcision than Mr. Booth has done?

But was it not, after all, a truly religious institution? Mr. Booth is not willing to deny this altogether. He seems to grant, at least by implication, that it was half a religious rite. "Baptism," says he, "is an appointment purely religious, for purposes entirely spiritual." By his using the words *purely* and *entirely* as applied to baptism, and then comparing it to circumcision, he seems to admit that circumcision was partly a religious rite. All he will grant in plain terms, concerning the religious nature of this institution is, that it "suggested spiritual instruction;" which is not peculiar to any rite either Jewish or Christian. I am sorry to see a man, of Mr. Booth's ability, trifle after this sort. He certainly knew not what to make of it; he saw something in its aspect dreadfully formidable to his system, and was afraid of its appearing, in that form, in which it is set forth in the word of God. These strokes in Mr. Booth's book, and such as these, which I intend to notice, convince me more than any thing I have ever read, of the fallacy of the Baptist's scheme.

Leaving Mr. Booth's erroneous account of this ordinance, we will view it as represented in the word of God. To see, then, whether it is a religious rite, we have only to view it, in its various relations to religion; and circumcision thus viewed will appear to have been of that description, as truly as baptism or the Lord's supper Let it be considered in its institution—in its application—in its obligation—and connexion with religious things.

1. In its institution. In this view of it, it was a token of God's covenant made with Abraham, in which he promised to be a God unto him, and his seed after him. And then, as an appendage, he promised to give him and his seed the land of Canaan for his temporal subsistence. For earthly things are appendages to the covenant of grace, they are things "added," as our Lord expresses it, to help a saint through this world.

2. We may view it further, in its application, under the threefold notion of a token, a sign, and a seal. As a token, it is a ratification of God's grant in covenant, to be a God to Abraham and his seed. As a sign, it denotes the grace of God on the heart, whereby it is enabled to love God, to worship him, and to have no confidence in the flesh. Deut. xxx. 6. Rom. ii. 28, 29. Phil. iii. 3. And therefore it is called a sign of circumcision, i. e. of the circumcision of the heart. As a seal, it applies to the righteousness of faith, i. e. the righteousness of Christ, by which men are justified.

3. We may consider it, in its connexion. And this is, with the Scriptures, Rom. iii. 2. "To them were committed the oracles of God." With the promises, Rom. xv. 8 "Now I say—that Jesus Christ was a min ister of the circumcision for the truth of God, to confirm the promises made unto the fa

thers." With baptism, Col. ii. 11, 12, wherein these two are spoken of as standing on a level with each other, as being each of them of the same religious kind.

If we view it in its obligation, we may observe, that as it was an entering into the visible church of God, so it bound the person, who received it, to a conformity to all other institutions, Gal. iii. 3. Without this conformity it profited nothing, for where this was wanting, it was deemed a nullity. That rite, therefore, which obliges to a conformity to religion, must be a religious rite.

When, therefore, we consider this institution, in its use and application, under all these views, there can be no doubt of its being a religious institution; because its whole use and application are so. And as nothing more can be said to prove the religious nature of baptism and the Lord's supper; a man might as well deny these to be religious ordinances, as the other. And hence it is that Mr. Booth's conduct is the more to be wondered at, who, notwithstanding he must have seen all this in Scripture, does, without authority from the word of God, transform it into a mere secular political rite. And this is done to destroy all analogy between it and baptism, for fear that analogy should prove the destruction of his scheme.

Mr. Booth in his preface says, *non tali auxilio, nec defensoribus istis.* This is to intimate to the reader, that a good cause does not need a bad defence. Now, if we are to form a judgment of the cause he has undertaken to support, from the means he makes use of, to support it, we cannot suppose the cause he has taken in hand, is any other than a very bad one. I question if a carnal Jew could have given a more frigid, degrading account of an institution of God, than he has done. According to him, it was only a sign of carnal descent—a mark of national distinction—a token of interest in temporal blessings—it had a political aspect—it was performed with political views—and (not knowing very well what to do with it, he introduces a learned word, and says) it was adapted to an ecclesiastico-political constitution. Thus he. But one thing he forgot—he has not given all this the sanction of the sacred text. Indeed, if it agree to any thing in the Bible, it agrees best of all to the circumcision of those poor Shechemites, who were first deceived and then destroyed by the sons of Jacob. Gen. xxxiv.

These two parts of the proposition being evinced; namely, 1. The church-membership of infants; and, 2. their admission to it, by a religious rite; the whole proposition which I undertake to maintain, and to lay as a ground-work, from which to conclude the baptism of infants, is this; God has constituted in his church the membership of infants, and has admitted them to it by a religious rite. Before I pass to the next argument, I will make a remark on each part.

I. From this fact, we learn so much of the

mind of God, as to be able to conclude, that there is nothing in a state of infancy, incompatible with church-membership. The reason is evident; for had there been any thing unsuitable in such a practice, God, who is an infinitely wise judge of decency and fitness, would never have ordained it. This conduct of the infinitely wise God, and the practice of about two thousand years, stand in direct repugnancy to the weak prejudice of Baptists; who, from the sentiment they have adopted, are led to suppose that there is nothing in nature more ridiculous, than the idea of infants being church members. This is one instance of human depravity, whereby the weakness of man sets itself up against the wisdom of God; and as this is the more to be admired in those persons, who in other respects are desirous of submitting to the whole will of God, so it serves to show, what a very unhappy influence the admission of an erroneous sentiment may gain over the mind.

II. It appears from this part of the divine conduct, in plain opposition to the views of Baptists, that the ignorance and want of faith, inseparable from a state of infancy, are no impediments to the administration of a religious ordinance; and this truth should be the more regarded by us, as it stands supported by the high authority of God; and is as a thousand arguments against all those pleas which are drawn from the incapacity of infants. For while we see those declared fit subjects of a religious ordinance, who could know nothing of its nature or use; with what prudence or piety can any man presume to affirm, that infants are incapable of such an ordinance? But if any one should take so much authority on himself, as to arbitrate against the wisdom of God, he would do well to consider, that God is true, and every man a liar, *i. e.* that judges differently.

ARGUMENT II.

The church-membership of infants was never set aside by God or man: but continues in force under the sanction of God, to the present day

THE force of this and the preceding argument taken together, may be comprehended by any man of common reasoning powers. Every one knows, that what was once done, and never undone, must of course remain the same: and that what was once granted, and never revoked, must needs continue as a grant. There can be no fallacy in all this. These arguments, therefore, being fairly maintained, will carry us forward, to a dilemma; and that dilemma will bring us home to the conclusion.

In good theory, the proof of this argument should not lie upon the Pædobaptist. For if I affirm, and prove, that God did settle a certain plan respecting church members, and another should come and affirm that that plan was now altered; it should lie on him to produce his proof that such an alteration has taken place; and the reason is, that whatever God has established should be supposed to continue, though we could bring no proof of its continuance, unless we are plainly told that he has ordered it otherwise. And then, since there is not a single text in Scripture to prove that the church-membership of infants is annulled, this argument should remain in force without further proof. However, I will waive this privilege, which I might justly claim, and proceed to evince the argument I have laid down.

There was only one point of time, in which it is even supposed that church-membership of infants was set aside; and that was, when the Gentiles were taken into a visible church state. In that period, several institutions did cease, and some new ones were ordained. Our only question is, whether the church-membership of infants did cease at the same time. It is evident that the mere change or cessation of institutions could work no change upon membership, any more than a man's having his clothes changed can produce a change upon the man. All institutions, whether typical or ratifying, that is, all institutions of every kind, are to be considered, in respect to church members, as means of grace, and nourishments for faith, respecting Christ the mediator, and the unsearchable riches of Christ; and then a change taking place in these things, will, in itself, produce no more alteration in the members of the church, than a change in a man's diet will destroy the identity of the man.

I am now to prove the church-membership of infants, which having been ordained of God, was never annulled, but carried forward into the Gentile church; and so consequently is in force at the present time. And this I shall proceed to do

From Scripture views of God's dispensation towards the Gentiles.

Much light might be thrown upon this subject, by considering those prophecies of the Old Testament, which relate to the calling in of the Gentiles. This Dr. Williams has done to great advantage: but my design being brevity, I shall confine myself to passages on that subject in the New Testament.

I. Matt. xxi. 43. "Therefore say I unto you, the kingdom of God shall be taken from you, and given to a nation bringing forth the fruits thereof."

The plain meaning of this passage is, that as, in times past, the church of God, which is his kingdom, was limited to Judea; so, in future, he would have a church in the Gentile world. The taking of the kingdom from the Jews, and giving it to the Gentiles, denotes,

1. The ceasing of a regular church state among the Jews. And this actually took place, by the destruction of some, and the dispersion of others, who did not receive the Lord Jesus Christ as sent of God; while

those who did receive him, were at length removed from Judea, and by degrees lost the name of Jew, in that of Christian. Rom. xi. 12.

2. The setting up a regular church state among the Gentiles. This, as the cessation of the church among the Jews, was gradually brought about. For the Gentiles who came over to Christ, joining themselves to the Jewish church, became in time the larger part. So that by the increase of the Gentiles, and the breaking off of the worthless branches among the Jews, nothing remained but an entire Gentile church.

3. The sameness of the church state among the Gentiles, with that among the Jews. For taking away and giving cannot import a change in the thing taken and given; but a transfer, the passing of a thing from one to the other. The kingdom given to the Gentiles was the same that was taken from the Jews: for all that was taken from the Jews was given to the Gentiles. Now, if we would know what was to be the church state among the Gentiles, we have only to learn what it had been among the Jews: for in both cases the church state was the same. And then, as it has before been proved, and admitted by the Baptists, that the church state among the Jews consisted in the membership of adults and infants, the church state among the Gentiles must consist of adults and infants too; because the same that was taken from the Jews was given to the Gentiles. And so it appears

from God's dispensation to the Gentiles, that the church-membership of infants was not set aside.—I will anticipate two objections in this place, which may be urged on each of the passages I shall allege.

1. It may be said, that in this way of viewing the subject, all the ordinances and rituals of the Jewish church must be adopted by the Gentile. To this I answer, that these things were not of the essence of a church state; but only means of grace, and helps to faith for the time being. Neither were these taken and given, but annulled; they were not transferred, but abolished. Rituals are to a church, as diet or ornaments are to a man; let the diet be changed, and the ornaments removed, the essence of the man will be still the same. So the state and essence of the church of God, before these rituals were ordained, and while they were in force, and after their abolition, was, and is, and must be, the same. This will be handled more fully in another place.

2. If any should say, it does not appear that women in the Jewish church were admitted to an initiating rite, and if so, there is a difference between the present church and the Jewish; I observe in answer, that this difference does not imply a removing or changing of any thing, but merely that of adding. That whereas the church state among the Jews included males both adult and infant; so to the Gentile church, together with these, there is, by the express order of God, the superaddition of females.

I would observe further, that the addition of females seems to me to be very favourable to the argument I am upon; because it is a new provision annexed to an old law. Now an alteration made in a law, gives an additional firmness to all those parts which are not altered. And the reason is, it supposes that all the unaltered parts are perfectly agreeable to the legislator's mind. And so, when the Lord expressly took away the partition between Jew and Gentile, and male and female, and passed over infants without making the least alteration in their case, he thereby gave a superadded confirmation, that the church-membership of infants, which had been before established, was in every respect agreeable to his will.

II. Rom. xi. 23, 24. "And they also, if they abide not still in unbelief, shall be grafted in again. for God is able to graft them in again. For if thou wert cut out of the olive-tree, which is wild by nature, and wert grafted contrary to nature into a good olive-tree; how much more shall these which be the natural branches, be grafted into their own olive-tree?"

1. The olive-tree is to denote a visible church state. 2. The Jews are said to be natural branches, because they descended from Abraham, to whom the promise was made. "I will be a God unto thee and to thy seed." 3. The Gentiles were brought into the same church state, from which the Jews were broken off. 4. The apostle suggests that the

Jews will again be grafted into their own olive-tree. From whence, with a view to my purpose, I would notice,

1. The future state of the Jews, who, he says, if they abide not in unbelief, shall be grafted in again. Grafting in again is the bringing of a person or thing into the same condition in which it was before. So the grafting in again of the Jews, is putting them into the same church state, in which they were before they were broken off. What was their church state before they were broken off. I answer, as before proved, that it consisted of the membership of adults and infants. Why then, if it before consisted of adults and infants, it will again consist of the same: because grafting in again is the placing of persons so grafted, in their former state. And that is in fact the same state, in which they would have continued, if they had never been broken off. That is, if it had not been for their unbelief, (for which they were cut off,) they would have continued, both they and their infants, as members of the church of God. So when it shall please God to give them faith, they will be reinstated, *i. e.* they and their infants will be members of the church of God again.

In compliance with this idea, I will just turn aside to observe, that it is natural for one error to lead to another; and that this is not more evident in any, than it is in the Baptists. They grant that infants were members of the Jewish church; and this from them is a very considerable concession. But a concession like this, leads to a consequence horribly alarming to their system. For if infants were once members of the church of God, then, it is evident, they were capable of such membership; and then the question will be, When did they cease to be members? and why are they not so now?

To remove this difficulty, the Baptists have recourse to this expedient. For as they cannot show from any place of Scripture, that infants are expressly set aside from church-membership; they fall to degrading the Jewish church, its membership and institutions: and when they have done, there is hardly any church or institution left. What was the Jewish church? Mr. Booth, vol. ii. 252. "It was an ecclesiastico-political constitution." What was the membership of it? Mr. Booth, page 251. "An obedient subject of their civil government, and a complete member of their church state, were the same thing." What was the church institution? Mr. Booth, page 250, &c. "It was a sign of carnal descent, a mark of national distinction; it had a political aspect, and was performed with political views." I wish I had a good casuist at my elbow, to explain what kind of church this could be. For had I been Mr. Booth, I would, to save trouble, have fairly denied that it was any church at all. And to say the truth of him, he has fairly done all this.

Now, it is a desperate cause, that leads a man to fall upon the very church of God.

But this is done to show that there is so great a difference between the church that now is, and that which once was, (or rather never was) that though infants were members of the one, they have no right, no capacity, to be members of the other.

This is one shift to ward off the consequence I have mentioned. But now we want another shift, to escape the consequence that is yet to come. "And they, if they abide not still in unbelief, shall be grafted in again." Grafting in again is the bringing of persons or things into their former condition. Now, if the former Jewish church state was all political, as Mr. Booth will have it, then the consequence will be, that when the Jews shall confess the Lord Jesus Christ, and believe with their heart, that God raised him from the dead, &c. and shall in consequence be re-ingrafted into their own olive-tree, they will be all political again! A mere ecclesiastico-political constitution! wherein an obedient subject of civil government, and a complete member of a church, will be the same thing! Well, when this shall take place, infant church membership may come about again.

But I return from this digression to notice,

2. The present state of the Gentiles. It appears from the text, that the church state is the same to the Gentiles, as it had been to the Jews, and as it will be to the Jews, in some future period, when it shall please God to graft them in again. And the reason of this is, because each in their turn belong to the

same olive-tree, *i. e.* the visible church state And therefore, as infants made a part of the church before the Jews were cut off, and will again make a part, when they shall be rein grafted; they must likewise make a part among the Gentiles: because the same olive-tree, *i. e.* church state, must confer the same privilege on all who shall be in it.

This truth will receive additional confirmation, and the contrary error will be more evident, if we consider, that since infants were once members among the Jews; and when their reingrafting shall take place, will be so again; so, if among the Gentiles they are deemed improper subjects of membership, and, in consequence of that, are universally rejected, two things will follow: 1. There will be, in the mean time, a very unhandsome schism in the ecclesiastical chain. For though infants were found members in the first ages of the church, and will be so in the last, there will be none to fill up the middle. And, 2. There will also be, in future time, a very unpleasant discordancy. For when the Jews shall be grafted in again, they will adopt their old practice of receiving infants to membership; while the Gentiles, denying they have any such right, will persist in shutting them out; and all this, as some suppose, in the spiritual reign of Christ.

III. Rom. xi. 17. "And if some of the branches be broken off, and thou being a wild olive-tree, were grafted in among them and with them partakest of the root and fatness of the olive tree; boast not thyself against the branches."

1. The olive-tree, as before noted, is the visible church state. 2. The branches are members of the visible church. 3. Some of these were broken off, and some remained. 4. The Gentiles who were called of God, were united to this remnant; for they were grafted in among them. From this view of the passage, I draw these three conclusions:

1. That there was no discontinuance of the ancient church state; in its essence, it remained the same as it had always been. That this is a true conclusion appears from hence; the text informs us that some of the branches were broken off; and if only some, then not all; and that remnant, continuing in their former state, constituted the still existing church of God. And then it follows, that as the church state continued as before, the membership of infants must likewise continue: because the membership of infants was a part of that church state. And this is the reason, that no new regulation, respecting infants, was made, or was necessary to be made; for all, who knew what God had ordained respecting membership, knew very well what to do with their infants, without any further information on that subject. This is the first conclusion, *viz.* that the ancient church state was not dissolved when the Gentiles were called in. And hence it follows,

2. That the bringing in of the Gentiles did not constitute a new church. This passage

informs us, that when the Gentiles were called in, they became members of the church already constituted: "They were grafted in among them," and so became one body, one fold; that " with them they might partake of the root and fatness of the olive-tree." The first Gentiles of whose calling we read, are said to have been added to the church; but there was no church existing to which they could be added, but the ancient Jewish church, of which all the apostles and disciples of our Lord were members. If the Gentiles, therefore, were added to the old church, or, as the text has it, were grafted in among them, and with them did partake of the root and fatness of the olive-tree, then it is evident, that the ancient church continued to exist, and no new one was formed at the calling in of the Gentiles. And then I conclude,

3. That infants were in a state of membership, in that very church to which the Gentiles were joined. And this must certainly be true, because they were grafted into that church, of which infants are, by the Baptists themselves, granted to have been members. And then, it is plain that infants made a part of that church, called by some the gospel church, the pure church of primitive apostolic times. This conclusion must needs be admitted, unless any one will affirm, that the ancient church state was entirely dissolved; or else, that the Gentiles were not united to this ancient church. And to affirm either of these, will be to affirm against the word of

God in general, and this text in particular. And herein the cause of the Baptists is ruined both ways; for if they maintain, that the old church was dissolved, and the Gentiles formed into a new one, their cause is ruined, by maintaining it against the word of God. But if they grant that the Jewish church continued, and that the Gentiles were grafted in among them, which is the real truth, then their cause is ruined that way. For then, as infants were in church-fellowship, in what is called the primitive apostolic church, it follows, that those societies, who admit infants to fellowship, act agreeably to the apostolic pattern; and consequently all those societies, who refuse to admit them, are in an error.

IV. Eph. ii. 14. " For he is our peace, who hath made both one, and hath broken down the middle wall of partition between us."

1. The terms [both and us] in this place, mean Jews and Gentiles. 2. A partition is that which separates one society or family from another. 3. It is said to have been broken down by Jesus Christ, who is called our peace, because he made peace by the blood of his cross. 4. The breaking down of a partition wall, brings the two societies, or families, into one. From this passage, the very same conclusions must be drawn as from the preceding:

1. That the Jewish church continued as before, and was not dissolved at the calling in of the Gentiles; and the reason is, the tak

ing down of a partition implies no dissolution of any society.

2. That the Gentiles were not formed into a new church: because the breaking down of a partition united them to the Jewish church, and "made both one."

3. The infants were in actual membership, in that church to which the Gentiles were united; because adults and infants being in fellowship among the Jews, the removal of the partition brought adults and infants into union with the Gentiles. And then, the point is clearly gained, namely, that infants hold the same place among the Gentiles, as they held before among the Jews.

I again affirm, that the point is evidently carried, unless one of these three things can be maintained: 1. That God excluded infants before the partition was taken down; or, 2. at the time it was taken down; or, 3. at some time after. For if one or other of these cannot be supported, then infants retain their right to church-membership to this day. Can any one maintain the first; that God excluded infants before the partition wall was broken down?—Upon what period will he fix?—And by what scripture will he support it?—Will any one affirm the third; that God excluded them after the partition was taken down?—I suppose not. For that would be granting that the Gentiles continued some time, *i. e.* till the exclusion took place in fellowship, in that church in which infants were members. And then, I might ask again, in what time did the expulsion take place? And where is it recorded in the word of God?—But I suppose, that he who contends for such an exclusion, will affirm the second; that infants were excluded at the time the partition wall was broken down. If so, I ask, who did exclude them? And how was it done? It could not be done by the mere taking down of the partition wall; for the taking down the partition unites those who before were separate, but does not exclude any.

But if they were excluded, it must be done either expressly or implicitly. The first is not true; for there is no express exclusion of infants in all the Scriptures. And the second will not do for a Baptist; for, as he will not admit implicit proof on the side of infants, so neither can he urge implicit proof against them. But let him take the advantage of implication; and say, that infants are excluded from church-membership, by all those places which require faith and repentance, &c. in order to baptism. To this I reply, that these places of Scripture can no more exclude infants from membership, than they exclude them from glory. And the fallacy of all this has been already fully evinced, when the second argument against infant baptism was considered: and to that part, for his satisfaction, I refer the reader. If, then, they were not excluded before the partition was taken down, nor at the time, nor at any time since, they were not excluded at all. And then the consequence will be, that infants, according to the will of God, are possessed of a right to church-fellowship under the present dispensation, and to the present day.

By these four passages, all relating to God's dispensation towards the Gentiles, it appears, that the church-membership of infants was left undisturbed, and was carried forward into the Gentile church; where it continues still the same as when first instituted. And the importance of this fact, in the present inquiry, is so very considerable, that whoever admits it, must be compelled to admit the right of infants to baptism, as a necessary consequence. Now, that God did ordain their church-membership has already been evinced, and granted by Baptists; and that to the present day, it has never been annulled, is what I am engaged to prove. I will, therefore, in addition to these four Scriptures, which of themselves clearly prove the fact, bring forward a variety of evidence, which serves to corroborate this important truth.

1. There is in the New Testament no law whatever to set aside the primitive right of infants to church-membership.

If a law could be found, in the New Testament, to repeal that which had been established in the Old, I grant freely, that all that has been said on the four places of Scripture, would signify nothing. But if no such law exist, the reasoning on the preceding passages will not only remain untouched, but will acquire a livelier force from that very fact. I need not prove to a Baptist, that the New Testament contains no law, by which infant membership is prohibited; he readily grants it; but adds in reply, that there was no necessity that such a law should be framed. Let us examine the thought.

If indeed nothing had been done respecting infants, this answer would have been a good one; but when the church-membership of infants is considered as an ancient establishment, the answer is nothing to the purpose. For as the case in reality stood, the want of a law to set aside infant membership left it in its original state, to continue down to the end of time. And how could it be otherwise? For who in this world was to alter it? It came down to Gentile times, in all the force an establishment can be supposed to have, or need to have, in order to its continuance. It had the precept of God— it had the partiality of parents—it had the practice of near two thousand years. If such an institution as this needed no law to set it aside, which is what the Baptists affirm; the true reason must be, because it was not the design of God it should be set aside. And what could have been a greater proof of the design of God to perpetuate it, than taking no measures to stop its progress? So that he, who grants that no such law was made, does in effect admit, that it is now a standing ordinance in the church of God, to receive infants to membership. And then he must grant too, that they should be baptized; because there is no other way of receiving them.

But though a Baptist admits there is no express law against their membership and baptism, yet he affirms that the requirement of faith and repentance does of itself exclude infants. This is the purport of the Baptists' second argument against infants, which I have proved to be a mere sophism. For when faith and repentance are required, in order either to baptism or salvation, a very easy distinction will make it plain, that infants are not excluded in either case. And this distinction is easy and obvious to every person.

1. It was a very easy one to a Jew. For while he knew that infants were received into the church by circumcision, he likewise knew that every adult who was circumcised, put himself under immediate obligation to confess his sins, to bring his sacrifice, and to conform to all the laws of that church. He was very sensible an infant could not do this; and yet he saw it right to circumcise the infant. So when he heard of faith, and repentance, and confession of sin, respecting baptism, as a medium of entering into the church, he had nothing to do but to use the same distinction, and all would be plain and easy as before.

2. The distinction is easy to a Pædobaptist. For he knows, that if the person be an adult, he must discover a disposition suited to the nature and design of the ordinance

but he knows, at the same time, that this was never designed to affect an infant, and that it can be no bar to his baptism, or blessedness.

3. This distinction is easy to a Baptist. For notwithstanding he is well persuaded, that he who believeth not shall not be saved, yet he knows an infant may be saved, though an infant do not believe. All this to him is easy and natural, and nothing in the world more plain. If this be so easy a distinction, it may be asked, why cannot a Baptist carry it to baptism, as well as to any thing else? I answer, he can if he please; for it arises from no defect of understanding that he does not do it;—but it is an unpleasant thing to employ a distinction, so as to destroy one's own sentiments.

In short, it is only considering, that an infant is not an adult, and that an adult is not an infant, than which nothing can be more easy; and then the requirement of faith and repentance is no more a law against the membership and baptism of infants, than it is against their salvation. All I meant here, was to affirm that there is no law, in the New Testament, to overrule the church-membership of infants; and this is a corroborating evidence, that their membership, which had been divinely instituted, continues the same down to the present time.

2. The Jews, at large, had no apprehension of the exclusion of infants; they neither oppose nor approve, which they doubtless

would have done, if such an exclusion had taken place.

This is a circumstance which merits particular attention, and has no small influence upon the present question. For as every material alteration in old customs is apt to stir up some opposition; so, had such a change as this been introduced, by which the infant offspring would have been put back from their former place in the church of God, it must have furnished occasion to a variety of animadversions: some, perhaps, might have been for it, while many would have opposed the new plan. That this would have happened, had such a revolution taken place, will appear still more certain, if we consider the nature of such a change, and the persons who would have felt themselves hurt by its introduction.

1. As to the change itself, it had a tendency to affect in a very sensible part. And this is a clear case, whether we consider the tender age of the subjects—or their number—or the privilege to which they were admitted—or the length of time through which the practice had been carried—or lastly, the divine authority which gave rise to that practice. Here is a practice of two thousand years' standing. The privilege was that of admitting infants to membership in the church of God—these infants formed a number in Israel exceedingly great. And this practice did not take its rise from some dark verbal or written tradition; but stood supported by

the lively oracles of God. Such was the custom which the Baptists suppose was annulled about this time.

2. On the other hand, if we take into consideration the character of those persons among whom this custom had prevailed, and among whom it is supposed to have ceased, we shall have sufficient reason to think it impossible that a custom of this nature should be abrogated, and they not oppose a single word. As to their character, it is certain, that, a few only excepted, they were, upon the whole, the deadly enemies of Christ and his doctrine. They were strongly attached to the forms and ceremonies of religion. They would wrangle for a rite, quarrel for a fast, and almost fight for a new moon. Every one knows what disturbance they made in the church of God, about such things as these.

Now is it possible, that such a change could be brought about, and among such a people, in a manner so still and silent, that in all the New Testament we do not read, that they ever said a word about it, for or against? No priest nor publican; no pharisee, lawyer, or libertine; neither pious nor profane; neither zealous, moderate, or lukewarm, in all the land of Israel, oppose a single sentence, or ask a reason why. But since this must have been a change so remarkable; and they among whom it is supposed to have happened, not the most modest; how came they to be so silent, so shy?

What made them so passive, so peaceable so complying? Nothing. They were neither complying, passive, nor peaceable, nor slow to speak, nor slow to wrath, when any old forms were invaded; but they were very much so about the change in question; and the true reason of it is, it never took place. There is another evidence, that the church-membership of infants was never annulled by God or man; and that is this:

3. Our Lord and his apostles take special notice of infants, and, instead of excluding them, they speak of them as still possessing a right to membership in the church of God.

The notice taken of infants by our Lord and his apostles, I call special; because it is not such as God takes of his creatures in a way of common providence; as the giving of food to a stranger, the satisfying the desire of every living thing, or hearing the cry of a young raven when he calls upon him. Such notice as this, God takes of all his creatures. But that which I now mean relates to matters of another nature, religious matters, the things of the kingdom of God, and our Lord Jesus Christ. The passages I shall bring are not intended to prove any new institution respecting infants, for nothing of this kind took place; but as their church-membership had been long settled, I only mean to show that our Lord speaks of them, under that idea, as the acknowledged members of the church of God. And hereby I mean to evince, that their membership, which had been long established, was never annulled to the present day. To this end I allege,

I. Luke ix. 47, 48. "And Jesus took a child, and set him by him, and ['when he had taken him in his arms,' Mark ix. 36.] he said unto them, Whosoever shall receive this child, in my name, receiveth me: And whosoever shall receive me, receiveth him that sent me: For he that is least among you all, the same shall be great." In this passage we have three things very observable:

1. The subject spoken of, a little child. There can be no doubt, but this was a child in regard of his age; as the circumstance of our Lord's taking him in his arms, makes this certain beyond dispute. And it is also evident, that what our Lord said did not apply to this child alone, as though something peculiar to himself led our Lord so to speak; since he makes it a thing general and common to other children. The words of Mark are, "Whosoever shall receive one of such children in my name." He meant, therefore, that child in his arms, and other little children like him.

2. The action respecting this child. "Whosoever shall receive this child in my name." To receive a person is to treat him suitably to his character, place, and station. John i. 11. "He came unto his own, and his own received him not." Rom. xiv. 1. "Him that is weak in the faith receive ye." To receive a person in the name of Christ, is to treat

him as one belonging to Christ, as one in visible union with him, as a member of that church, of which he is the head. Matt. x. 40. " He that receiveth you, receiveth me; and he that receiveth me, receiveth him that sent me." This is spoken of the apostles of Christ, and intends a treatment suitable to their character, and the relation they stood in to him. So John xiii. 20. Then the meaning is, Whosoever shall receive this child, or one of such children, in my name, *i. e.* as persons belonging to me, and in visible union with myself, receiveth me, *i. e.* treateth me as the visible head of the church of God.

Whosoever shall receive this child, or one of such children, in my name! Remarkable phrase! I have pondered it in my own mind, and wish to submit it to any casuist, with this question: is it possible to receive a person in the name of Christ, without considering that person as visibly belonging to Christ? I own, that to me, it appears impossible. But as Christ knows best what his own words imply, he shall determine the question. Mark ix. 41. " Whosoever shall give you a cup of water to drink in my name, because ye belong to Christ." So to give to any in his name, is to give to them, because they belong to Christ. And then, when Christ speaks of receiving little children in his name, we are to consider little children as visibly belonging to him. And if they visibly belong to him, who is

OF INFANT BAPTISM. 81

Head of the church, it is because they visibly belong to that church, of which he is Head.

3. The reason of this action. This reason is twofold: 1. As it respected God and Christ; "Whosoever shall receive this child in my name, receiveth me; and whosoever receiveth me, receiveth him that sent me." The force of the reason lies in this; receiving little children in Christ's name, *i. e.* treating them as visibly belonging to him, is showing a proper regard to God and Christ. But why should this be considered as showing a proper regard to God? I answer, I know no reason in the world but one: and that is, because God had long before constituted infants visible members of his own church, and still continued to them the same place and privilege. 2. As it respected themselves. "He that is least among you all, the same shall be great." This reason suggests three things: 1. our Lord speaks of his disciples, in a collective capacity, as forming a religious society or church; "He that is least among you all." And this, indeed, was truly the case; for these disciples, with others, were branches in the olive-tree; and such branches as were not broken off. 2. Our Lord speaks of them, as having little children in their society or church; 'He that is least among you all, the same shall be great." Now, though it is true, that adults on some accounts may be called little children, yet the term [least] cannot mean adults in this place; because this is

given as a reason why they should receive this little child. For what God will do for an adult can be no motive to the receiving an infant. If we say, God can make that adult, which you deem very little, to become great; therefore receive this little child: this would be no reason at all. But if it be taken thus; God can make the least child in your community to become great, therefore receive this little child; the reasoning will be good, and becoming the wisdom of Christ. And this is no more than a plain fact; children were at this time the acknowledged members of the church of God. 3. Our Lord speaks thus, to induce them to pay a proper regard to children. "The least among you shall become great; therefore receive this child in my name." Receiving may respect the first act of recognizing a person a member of a church; or all subsequent acts, by which we treat them as such. Our Lord's expression is applicable to both, and enjoins both on his disciples. This is one instance of special notice taken of infants, in which they are considered as holding a place in the church of God.

Mark x. 14. "But when Jesus saw it, he was much displeased, and said unto them, Suffer the little children to come unto me, and forbid them not: for of such is the kingdom of God."

The persons who were brought, are said by Mark to have been "young children," our Lord calls them "little children," and Luke calls them "infants." There can be no doubt but they were such as were in an infantile state. The design, for which they were brought, is said to be, that he should put his hands on them, and pray. Some of the Baptists *suppose* they were diseased children, and were brought to our Lord to be healed; but of this there is nothing said. It is most likely they were brought to receive the benediction of Christ. Mark x. 16.

That this passage regards infants, as continuing in a state of church-membership, which is all I produce it for, will appear by considering of whom our Lord spake, and what he spake of them.

1. Of whom he spake. There can be very little difficulty on this part of the subject, as we are plainly told, what the persons were who were brought to him, and of whom it is evident he spake. Some of the Baptists remarking upon the phrase *tōn toioutōn*, of such, or of such like, affirm that our Lord meant adults of a child-like disposition, and that of these, and not of the infants, he said, Of such is the kingdom of God. This construction, which indeed has nothing to support it, will appear very uncouth, when we consider these words of our Lord, as a reason for bringing and permitting the little children to come to him: suffer them to come unto me, for of such is the kingdom of God. But this exposition, besides that it makes our Lord speak obscurely, represents him as giving a reason quite distant from the subject he

was upon. For whereas a reason for coming should be taken from those who are to come, and not from others; this exposition makes our Lord say, Suffer *these* to come, because *those* belong to the kingdom. To say, adults belong to the kingdom of God, is no good reason for bringing infants to Christ. It is a much better one to say, Suffer these little children to come, because these little children, and others like them, belong to the kingdom of God. But if it be said, others belong to the kingdom of God, because they are like infants, then infants must belong to the kingdom of God because they are like them. The truth is, our Lord evidently speaks of infants as he had done before, in the preceding passage.

2. What he spake of them: of such is the kingdom of God; that is, such belong to the kingdom. Our inquiry is, what kingdom did our Lord mean? was it the church, or a state of glory? If the Lord meant the church, then he has asserted what I contend for, that infants were spoken of by him, as members of the church; and, therefore, the fact is established. But the Baptists in general understand this of a state of glory, and allow infants to belong to that, but deny that they belong to the church. This, indeed, is granting the greater, and denying the less; and therefore an argument may be taken, from what they grant, to destroy what they deny; that is, an argument *a majore ad minus*, from the greater to the less. If infants belong to

a state of glory, which is the greater; then much more do they belong to a church-state, which is the less. Besides, as the institution of a church is a dispensation of God, which leads to glory, it is absurd to grant persons a place in glory, and at the same time deny them a place in that dispensation which leads to it.

Though to affirm, that our Lord, by the kingdom of God, intended a state of glory, does not militate against, but rather concludes for the church-membership of infants; there are some considerations which serve to evince that our Lord intended the church on earth chiefly, if not only; for I have some doubt whether he did not intend both, though the church more particularly. It is to be observed, in the first place, that these words, "of such is the kingdom of God," were spoken to the apostles, as a reason for their suffering, and a rebuke for their hindering, little children to come unto him. Now it is always more natural, when we intend to reason with, or rebuke any person, to fix upon that as a reason, which is most familiar to him. The apostles were well acquainted with the membership of infants in the church, as a practice which had prevailed in their nation for many centuries; whereas they could know but little of the state of infants with respect to glory. Now as the reason, why these little children should be suffered to come, was, that they belonged to the kingdom of God; and as this was designed, at the same time, as a rebuke;

it must be evident, that our Lord intended that idea of the kingdom with which they were most familiar. For had it been meant of a state of glory, the apostles might very well have pleaded ignorance; but they could not be ignorant that infants belonged to the church, and therefore the reproof could not come home to them, but under that idea. For in that, they acted contrary to a principle they knew, in keeping those, who belonged to the church, from the church's Head.

It may be further remarked, that it is highly reasonable to conclude, that our Lord intended the same reason, for infants coming to him, as he had urged to others, for their receiving them. Others were to receive infants in his name; and with this to enforce it, that whosoever received them in his name, received him, &c. This expression denotes a relation to himself; as if he had said, Receive them, because they belong to me, receive them as you would a disciple. This is a reason that has respect to present relation; and if it be natural to suppose, that our Lord gives a similar reason for their coming to him, the kingdom of God will not mean a future state of blessedness, but a present church state, to which they belong. Moreover, it may be said with much more truth of infants in general, and it is of such our Lord speaks, that they belong to a church on earth, than to a state of glory; because many may belong to the former who do not belong to the latter. And whereas it cannot be said of infants, as such, that they belong to a state of glory, for then all would be saved, because all have been infants; but it could be said of infants, as infants, where our Lord was, that they belonged to the church on earth.

I only introduce this to show, that our Lord, in saying, Of such is the kingdom of God, did recognize infants as church-members. And against this sense of the kingdom, as meaning the church, the Baptists bring only one objection, *viz.* the incapacity of infants. But this is removed by the practice of many centuries; which shows that God does not judge of incapacity, after the manner of men. What our Lord said, as it proves the membership of infants, which is all I brought it for, so it is no more than what was familiar to the whole nation.

Acts ii. 38, 39. " Then Peter said unto them, Repent and be baptized every one of you in the name of Jesus Christ; for the remission of sins, and ye shall receive the gift of the Holy Ghost. For the promise is unto you, and to your children, and to all that are afar off, even as many as the Lord our God shall call."

As this passage is only brought forward to show, that infants are spoken of in the New Testament, as church-members, agreeable to the ancient dispensation of God; I shall confine myself to these three conclusions:

I. That the phrase, " to you, and to your children," intends adults and infants.

II. That this promise must comprehend

adults and infants, wherever it comes, even as long as God shall continue his word to us.

III. That infants are placed in the same relation to baptism, as they were of old to circumcision.

These I shall now proceed to evince; and in the first place I affirm.

I. That the phrase, To you and to your children, intends adults and infants. This may be proved by considering,

1. The resemblance between this promise and that in Gen. xvii. 7. " To be a God unto thee, and unto thy seed after thee." The resemblance between these two lies in two things; 1. Each stands connected with an ordinance, by which persons were to be admitted into church-fellowship; the one by circumcision, the other by baptism.

Both agree in phraseology; the one is, " to thee, and to thy seed;" the other is, " to you and to your children." Now every one knows that the word " seed" means children; and that children means seed; and that they are precisely the same. From these two strongly resembling features, *viz.* their connexion with a similar ordinance, and the sameness of the phraseology, I infer, that the subjects expressed in each, are the very same. And as it is certain that parents and infants were intended by the one; it must be equally certain that both are intended by the other.

2. The sense, in which the speaker must have understood the sentence in question. The promise is, to you and to your children.

In order to know this, we must consider who the speaker was, and from what source he received his religious knowledge. The Apostle, it is evident, was a Jew, and brought up in the Jewish church. He knew the practice of that church, with respect to those who were admitted to be its members. He knew, that he himself had been admitted in infancy, and that it was the ordinary practice of the church to admit infants to membership. And he likewise knew, that in this they acted on the authority of that place, where God promises to Abraham, "to be a God unto him, and to his seed." Now if the Apostle knew all this; in what sense could he understand the term children, as distinguished from their parents? I have said, that children, [*tekna*] and seed, [*sperma*] mean the same thing. And as the Apostle well knew, that the term seed intended infants, though not mere infants only; and that infants were circumcised, and received into the church, as being the seed; what else could he understand, by the term children, when mentioned with their parents? Those who will have the Apostle to mean, by the term children, adult posterity only, have this infelicity attending them, that they understand the term differently from all other men; and this absurdity that they attribute to the Apostle a sense of the word, which to him must have been the most unfamiliar and forced. And, therefore, that sense of the word for which they contend, is the most unlikely of all to be the true one, because it is utterly improbable that a person should use a word in that sense which to him, and to all the world beside, was altogether unfamiliar.

3. In what sense his hearers must have understood him, when he said, "The promise is to you, and to your children."

The context informs us, that many of Peter's hearers, as he himself was, were Jews. They had been accustomed for many hundred years to receive infants, by circumcision, into the church; and this they did, as before observed, because God had promised to be a God to Abraham, and to his seed. They had understood this promise, to mean parents and their infant offspring; and this idea was become familiar by the practice of many centuries. What then must have been their views, when one of their own community says to them, "The promise is to you, and to your children?" If their practice of receiving infants was founded on a promise exactly similar, as it certainly was; how could they possibly understand him, but as meaning the same thing, since he himself used the same mode of speech? This must have been the case, unless we admit this absurdity, that they understood him in a sense to which they had never been accustomed.

How idle a thing it is, in a Baptist, to come with a lexicon in his hand, and a criticism in his head, to inform us that *tekna*, children, means posterity! Certainly it does, and so it means the youngest infants. The verb *tikto*, from which it comes, signifies to bring forth, *i. e.* the offspring. And are not infants of that number? But the Baptists will have it that *tekna*, children, in this place, means only adult posterity. And, if so, the Jews to whom he spoke, unless they understood him in a way in which it was morally impossible they should, would infallibly have understood him wrong. Certainly all men, when acting freely, will understand words in that way which is most familiar to them; and nothing could be more familiar to the Jews, than to understand such a speech, as Peter's, to mean adults and infants. So that if the Jews, the awakened Jews, had apprehended the Apostle to mean only adults, when he said, "To you and your children;" they must have had an understanding of such a peculiar construction, as to make that sense of a word, which to them was totally unnatural and forced, to become familiar and easy.

We should more certainly come at the truth, if, instead of idly criticising, we coul l fancy ourselves Jews, and in the habit of circumcising infants, and receiving them into the church. And then, could we imagine one of our own nation and religion, to address us in the very language of Peter in this text, "The promise is to you and your children;" let us ask ourselves, as in the sight of God, whether we could ever suppose him to mean adult posterity only? Or if, instead of putting ourselves in the situation of

Jews, we should suppose the Apostle to address the members of the Church of England, in the same phraseology, as he did the Jews, can any person doubt, whether they would understand him to mean adults and infants? It is certainly impossible. And why? Because they have been for ages in the habit of receiving infants into the church. Just so it was with the Jews when the apostle addressed them; and, therefore, they could no more have understood him, as meaning to exclude infants, than the members of the Church of England would by the use of the same phrase.

I have been endeavouring to prove that both Peter, who spoke, and the Jews, who were his hearers, must have understood the promise in the text to mean adults and infants; because such a meaning would be to them the most natural and obvious, both from their own habit and practice, and from its exact resemblance to that promise on which their practice was founded, and by which their habit was formed. But since Mr. Booth and all the Baptists will have it to mean no such thing, I shall only say, as Mr. Booth does in his answer to Dr. Williams, page 274, " Then Dr. Samuel Johnson might well say, though a man, accustomed to satisfy himself with the obvious and natural meaning of a sentence, does not easily shake off his habit, yet a true-bred lawyer never contents himself with this sense when there is another to be found." " My opponent," says Mr. Booth to Dr. Williams, " seems to have imbibed the spirit of Dr. Johnson's true-bred lawyer; for he cannot be at all content with the obvious and natural meaning, &c." *Mutato nomine, &c.* This is true of Mr. Booth. —I am to prove in the next place,

II. That this promise must comprehend adults and infants wherever it comes, let it come wherever it may.

The Apostle, in applying this promise, distinguishes those to whom it is to apply into present and absent. The first class were his hearers; the second he describes two ways— all that are afar off—as many as the Lord our God shall call. To each of these classes, *viz.* those who were present, and those who were absent, he applies the promise in the text. To those who were present, the promise is, to you and to your children;—to those afar off, and the promise is to you and to your children;—to as many as the Lord our God shall call, the promise is to you and to your children. Let the promise come to what persons soever it may, it must come to them and to their children; because the promise must be the same wherever God shall send it. I have already proved that the words, you and your children, mean adults and infants; and both being in the promise, it must therefore belong to each: to you adults and to your infants, who are present; to you adults, who are afar off, and to your infants; to as many adults as the Lord our God shall call, and their infants. That this is true may be proved by considering the essence or nature of the promise.

There are two things which enter into the essence of a promise: it must contain some good—it must be made to some person or persons. That these two belong to the essence of a promise appears by this, that if either be taken away, there can be no promise—*e. g.* I will be a God to thee and to thy seed; the good in this promise is God himself—the persons were Abraham and his seed. If the good be taken away, it will then be no promise; I will—to thee and to thy seed. The case will be the same if the persons are taken away; I will be a God—in either case it is no promise. So when a promise is made to different persons, one person is as essential to the promise as the other—*e. g.* I will be a God unto thee and to thy seed; the promise is as much to the seed as to Abraham, and as much to Abraham as to the seed; because both are essential to the promise.

Now the Apostle, expressing the essence or nature of the promise in the text, as it respects the objects, says, "The promise is to you and to your children." Both parts, therefore, belong to the promise; it is essential to the promise that it be—to you;—it is likewise essential to it that it be to your children. And the case being so, we cannot take away either part without violating the essence of the promise. We have no more right to say, The promise is to you, but not to your children, than the promise is to your children, but not to you; for as it was the design of God that the promise should be to both, it was his design that it should be to their children as truly as to themselves. And so the promise must be to Peter's hearers and their children—to all that are afar off, and to their children—to as many as the Lord our God shall call, and to their children, and the reason is, both enter into the essence of the promise. So when God said, "I will be a God unto thee and to thy seed," it would apply, in the same form, "to thee and to thy seed," to every man and every generation of men of the offspring of Abraham, as long as the promise was in force.

Mr. Booth objects to this, in vol. ii. p 355, and says, "These words [as many as the Lord our God shall call] are, as plainly as possible, a limiting clause, and extend a restrictive force to the term, children, as much as to the pronoun, you, or to that descriptive language, all that are afar off." To this I reply, that the apostle himself did not make use of that limit which Mr. Booth says is so plain; for the apostle actually spoke to those who, in Mr. Booth's sense, were already awakened and called; and then, as plainly as possible, distinguishes between them and their children. Now if the apostle addressed those who were already called, and extended the promise beyond them, even to their children then the promise was not limited to the called. But this the apostle actually did, as plainly as words could express it; for he spoke to those who were pricked in their heart, and said, "Men and brethren, what shall we do?" To these he said, "The promise is unto you," and, instead of confining it to them only, he extends it to their children also; and so passes over that limit which Mr. Booth is pleased to lay down. And as the apostle extends the promise beyond the called, in the first clause, we must follow his example, and extend it beyond the called in the last clause. Thus the promise is to as many as the Lord our God shall call, and to their children: and then Mr. Booth's limiting clause will be nothing more than a very lame evasion.

Notwithstanding this, there is some truth in Mr. Booth's idea respecting the limiting clause, though he himself, by misapplication, has done violence to that truth. That clause "to as many as the Lord our God shall call," is really a limiting clause, but not in the way Mr. Booth supposes. This, like every other promise, has two limits, and these two are fixed by two limiting clauses: one limit determines how wide the promise shall extend; the other how far it is to run—the one is a limit of latitude, the other of longitude. The limit of latitude extends to parents and children—that of longitude reaches down "to as many as the Lord our God shall call." And as there is a perfect harmony between these two, there is no need to destroy the one in order to preserve the other; for both limits being settled and fixed, that of latitude which ex-ends to parents and children, must continue firm, till, through successive ages, it comes down to that of longitude, which reaches to as many as the Lord our God shall call; that is, as long as God shall continue to call, the promise shall pertain to parents and children.

Mr. Booth therefore, was very right in making this a limiting clause, for so it really is; but he was very wrong when, instead of preserving both, he set one limit to destroy the other. And as it often falls out that those, who do violence to the spirit of a text, are led to utter some rash expression against the letter of it, just so it has fallen out in Mr. Booth's case. He has violated one limit in the text, and has so expressed himself as to exceed all limits. In vol. ii. p. 354, he has said, " There is nothing said about the promise respecting any besides those who were then awakened." Those who were awakened, are distinguished by the pronoun " you;" and it is certain something is said about the promise respecting them. But, says Mr. Booth, " There is nothing said about the promise respecting any besides." Mr. Booth should not have said this with the text before his eyes. He should first have erased that clause of it, " and to your children," and not have left it stand to contradict him. As something was said about the promise respecting those who were awakened, and their children both, he might as well have denied it respecting the wakened, as to deny it respecting their children; but it is often the fate of those who oppose truth, to lose truth and modesty together.

When any dispute happens on a place of Scripture, and it cannot be settled from the context, the best way is to pass to a similar place, and observe (if there be any plain indications) in what manner that was understood, and what practice took place upon it. That passage, to which the text bears the strongest resemblance, is Genesis xvii. 7. "I will establish my covenant—to be a God unto thee and to thy seed." There is no place in Scripture so like the text as this; they are both worded in the same way—"to thee and to thy seed"—"to you and to your children." They are both connected with a religious ordinance. By seed, which is the same as children, was meant an infant of eight days old and upwards; and because a promise is made to the seed, an infant becomes the subject of a religious ordinance. Now, if the language of the text be similar, and if it be connected with a religious ordinance, as that was, what better comment can be made upon it, than what that passage suggests? Why should not the ideas be alike, if the language and circumstances be so? The reason why a comparing of Scripture with Scripture assists the understanding, is this: when God uses the same kind of language in two places of Scripture, and the circumstances are alike, it is plain he means to be understood as intending similar things. This is so sure a rule of interpretation, that we are not afraid of venturing our everlasting interests upon it: and, by adopting it in this instance, the result will be clearly this. that the Holy Ghost, by the phrase, "you and your children," meant adults and infants; that these are placed together in the same promise; and that the promise, thus made to adults and infants, is connected with baptism. And from hence it may be proved,

III. That infants are placed in the same relation to baptism, as they were of old to circumcision.

Let any one compare the two places together, *viz.* Gen. xvii. 7. 9, 10, and this now before us, and he will see that parents and children are united, in each promise, in the same way—there the promise is, "to thee and to thy seed"—here it is, "to you and to your children;"—that the promise, in each place, is connected with a religious ordinance. In Genesis it is connected with circumcision—in this text with baptism;—that in both places, the ordinance is made to result from the promise—the one is set down as a reason for the other; Gen. xvii. 9. " Thou shalt keep my covenant therefore;" that is, because God had given a promise. So here, " Repent, and let every one of you, of yours be baptized, for (*gar*, because) the promise is to you and to your children." Infants, therefore, in this passage, are placed in the same relation to baptism as they were anciently to circumcision. This being so, I reason thus:

When a positive institution is connected with a promise, all, who are contained in the promise, have a right to the institution. I think any one may be compelled to grant this, as it is certainly an undeniable truth; for if parents must, therefore, be circumcised because they are included in the promise, then, as infants are also included in the promise, they too must be circumcised. All this is evinced by the history of circumcision, and is indeed a self-evident case; because if a promise give a right to an institution, the institution must belong to all who are interested in the promise. And, therefore, we may reason thus: if parents must be baptized because the promise belongs to them, then must their infants be baptized, because the promise is to them also. This mode of reasoning is the more certain, as it is confirmed, beyond all doubt, by the divine procedure; for if you ask, Who were to be circumcised? the reply is, Those to whom the promise was made. If you inquire again, to whom was the promise made? we answer, To adults and infants. Again, if you ask, Who are to be baptized? the answer is, Those to whom the promise is made. But to whom is it made? The apostle says, "To you and to your children." Now what proof more direct can be made or desired for infant baptism?

From these premises the result is plainly this: that as infants stand, in this text, in the same relation to baptism as they did to

OF INFANT BAPTISM. 101

circumcision, their right to the one must be the same as it was to the other. The case, in both instances, stands fairly thus: the promise connects itself with the ordinance; that with circumcision—this with baptism. It also connects two parties together, infants and parents, and unites them both to that ordinance with which itself is connected. It is by virtue of the union of the promise with the ordinance, that those who have an interest in the one have a right to the other; and when two parties, parents and children, are interested in the same promise, and that promise gives a right to the ordinance, it gives the same right to both the parties who are interested in it. And hence, as parents and children are interested in the promise, the right of the children to the ordinance is the same as that of parents.

I produce these three passages only to show, that special notice is taken of infants, and that they are spoken of agreeably to the idea of their church-membership. In Luke ix. 47, 48, our Lord proposes them for reception in his name, and thereby owns them as visibly related to himself. He indicates that the reception was to be of the same kind as that which might be claimed by his own disciples; and that receiving them as visibly related to himself, *i. e.* in his name, was showing a proper respect to him, and to his Father who sent him: " whosoever shall receive this child in my name, receiveth me; and whosoever shall receive me, receiveth him that sent me," &c. In Mark x. 14, our Lord explicitly declares what was the ground of that reception, by expressing their visible relation to the church, and so to himself:—"Of such is the kingdom of God;" as such they were to be brought to him, and no one was to forbid them to come. In Acts ii. 38, 39, infants are placed in the same relation to baptism as they were before to circumcision. The apostle unites them with their parents in the promise, and connects that promise with baptism; thereby copying the divine pattern in Genesis xvii. and allotting them the same station with respect to baptism, as they had before with regard to circumcision.

In each of these cases infants are spoken of agreeably to that constitution of God, by which they were admitted to church-membership, and to a religious ordinance. And this being all that my argument requires, I shall proceed to notice one thing more, *viz.*

IV. The historical account of the baptism of households as recorded in the Scripture.

The instances of this kind are three; the family of Lydia, Acts xvi. 15; the family of the jailer, Acts xvi. 33; and that of Stephanas, 1 Cor. i. 16. The case of the jailer and his family is thus described: "and he took them the same hour of the night, and washed their stripes, and was baptized, he and all his, straightway. And when he had brought them into his house, he set meat before them, and rejoiced, believing in God, with all his house, *eegalliasato panoiki pepisteukôs tō Theō.*" He rejoiced domestically, believing in God; *i. e. he,* believing in God, rejoiced over his family. Now, as the household of the jailer is expressed by the phrase, "all his, or all of his," it explains the term *Oikos,* household, or family, which is used in the two other instances: so then, to baptize a man's household is to baptize all his. This may serve as a pattern of primitive practice—he and all his were baptized. But whether all believed, or were capable of believing, is not said, no mention being made of any one's faith but his own. And though I do not consider this historic account as having force enough of itself to evince the baptism of infants, yet there are two considerations which give it weight on that side.

(1.) Its agreement with that practice, in which we are sure infants were included: I mean the practice of Abraham, and the Jews, with respect to circumcision. This agreement may be considered, 1. In the principle which led to the practice. Circumcision was founded on this promise of God, "I will —be a God unto thee, and to thy seed." Baptism proceeds on this, that the promise is to you and to your children; and in this they are both alike. 2. In the practice itself. When Abraham received circumcision, his household were circumcised with him; so when the jailer was baptized, all his were baptized likewise. Now, when we discern two cases alike in principle and practice, and are sure that infants were included in the one we then very naturally are led to conclude, that infants must be intended in the other.

(2.) Its accordance with the hypothesis of infant baptism. Such accounts as these have a favourable aspect on the sentiments of Pædobaptists; because on their plan, provided they were placed in the same circumstances as the apostles were, whose lot it was to preach the gospel where Christ had not been named; cases of a like nature would very frequently occur. Whereas, on the plan of the Baptists, if placed in similar circumstances, though we might hear of various persons baptized on a profession of faith; we should not expect to hear of the baptizing of households; or, that any man, and all his, were baptized straightway. And indeed, the very idea of baptizing households, and of a man, and all his, being baptized at the same time, does so naturally fall in with the views of Pædobaptists, that I am inclined to think it passes with the common people, instead of a hundred arguments. For though they do not reason by mood and figure, neither do they confine themselves to logical accuracy, in any form; yet they have logic enough to see, that the baptizing of a man, and all his, and likewise of this and the other household, is by no means agreeable to the plan, and that it has no resemblance to the practice of the Baptists.

It is in this way, I consider these accounts of baptizing as having weight in the present inquiry. Here are facts recorded, relative to baptizing; I take these facts, and compare them with the proceedings of different baptizers; and I find they will not agree to one class, but very well with the other: I, therefore, am led to conclude, that that class of baptizers agree best to the primitive practice, to whom these facts will best agree. For, as the practice of the apostles has no affinity with that of the Baptists, it is very reasonable to infer, that their views of the subject could not be the same.

This being the last corroborating argument I mean to bring, I will collect the force of the whole into one view. The whole defence of infants rests on two arguments;—1. That God did constitute in his church the membership of infants, and admitted them to it by a religious ordinance. 2. That the right of infants to church-membership was never taken away: the consequence of which is, that their right to membership continues to the present moment. The first of these arguments is granted by the Baptists themselves. The other I have evinced from five topics: 1. From God's dispensation towards the Gentiles, in forming them into a church state. 2. That God never did, by any law, take away that right which had been before granted to infants. 3. That none of the Jews had any apprehension of the rejection of infants, which they must have had, if infants had been rejected. 4. That Jesus Christ spake of them as visibly belonging to the church, and to himself, as the Head of the church: and that the apostle Peter placed them in the same relation to baptism, as they had been before to circumcision. 5. That the apostle Paul, in baptizing whole families, acted agreeably to, and so evinced the validity of, all the preceding arguments.

The evident result of the whole is, that infants, according to divine appointment, have a right to church-membership, to the present hour. Then, the only question that remains, and by answering of which, I shall be brought to the close of the inquiry, is this: have infants (any infants, for I take them indefinitely) any right to Christian baptism? To this I reply, 1. That those persons who have a right to be members, should certainly be admitted to membership; *i. e.* solemnly recognized. And the reason is, because every one should have his right. 2. If persons, who have a right to be members, should be received to membership; then they are to be received, either without baptism, or with it. I suppose none will say, they are to be received without baptism; for then, if one may be so received, so may all, and thus baptism will be excluded. I expect no opposition from a Baptist in this place. For if the right of infants to membership be once evinced, the opposition of a Baptist is over. And therefore, if he be able to do any thing in this controversy, it must be done before it comes to this. On the other hand, if no person is to be received to membership without baptism; then every one who should be received, must of necessity be baptized. And so the conclusion of the whole will be this : since infants, therefore, have a right to membership, and all who have such right must be received as members, and none should be received without being baptized; then it follows, that as infants have a right to be received, they must also have a right to be baptized; because they cannot be received without baptism.

CHAPTER III.

Having advanced what I judged essential on both sides, I will now, agreeably to my design, give the reader a scheme of the whole. By this scheme the reader will be able to discover what is common to both sides, and what is the force of each. It was in this way, the subject presented itself to my mind, when I was led a second time to take it under consideration. And I persuade myself, that, by adopting this method, the reader will be more capable of judging, in this controverted question, which side of the two is the stronger, and consequently which is the true one. I will place the whole on one page, that the reader may have it at once under his eye. I shall place those Scriptures, that weigh equal on both sides, at the top of the page; and the arguments against infant baptism in one column, and those for their baptism in the other. I do this, because I know of no method more fair, or more calculated to lead to the truth as it is in Jesus.

A Scheme of the Controversy on Baptism.

I. Those places of Scripture which are common to both sides, *viz.* Baptists and Pædobaptists. Matt. iii. 6. "And were baptized of him in Jordan, confessing their sins." Mark xvi. 16. "He that believeth and is baptized shall be saved." Acts ii 41. "Then they that gladly received his word, were baptized." Acts viii. 27. "And Philip said, If thou believest with all thine heart, thou mayest," &c.

N. B. *These places, and others of the same kind, as they prove the baptism of an adult to be right, are expressive of the sentiment of Baptists and Pædobaptists, with respect to an adult subject: For both think it right to baptize an adult. And as they prove equally on both sides, they cannot be urged by either party against the other.*

II. Those arguments which are peculiar to each, compared.

N. B. *The question is not of adults; in this both are agreed: " But, Are infants to be baptized?"*

ARGUMENTS AGAINST INFANT BAPTISM.

1 Whoever has a right to a positive ordinance must be expressly mentioned as having that right; but infants are not so mentioned, with respect to baptism: Therefore infants are not to be baptized.

2. The Scriptures require faith and repentance in order to baptism; but infants have not faith or repentance: Therefore infants are not proper subjects of baptism.

ARGUMENTS FOR INFANT BAPTISM.

1 God has constituted in his church the membership of infants, and admitted them to it by a religious rite.

2. The church-membership of infants was never set aside by God or man; and consequently continues in force to the present day.

N B. *The Baptists admit the first. The other is, by a variety of evidence, clearly evinced.*

Coroll.—*As God has constituted infants church members, they should be received to membership, because God has constituted it.*

Dilemma.—*Since infants must be received to membership, they must be received without baptism, or with it: But none must be received without baptism; and, therefore, as infants must be received, they must of necessity be baptized.*

I shall now only make a few remarks on this scheme of the controversy, and so conclude this part of the subject.

1. At the top of the page, I have cited some passages of Scripture, which support the sentiment of both parties, that is, the propriety of baptizing an adult professing faith, &c. These, and such like Scriptures, which for want of room I have not set down, prove as much on one side as on the other; and, therefore, I have said they are common to both parties. My design in placing them at the head of the scheme, is to detect an error incident to Baptists in general; namely, a supposition that such texts prove only on their side, and against the sentiments of Pædobaptists. I have observed this error, in every Baptist with whom I have conversed, both before and since my present sentiments have been known. I once asked a worthy Baptist minister, what he thought were the strongest arguments against Pædobaptists? He immediately had recourse to such passages as are set down in the scheme. I told him, that these were so far from being the strongest, that they were no arguments at all against Pædobaptists; but rather proved on their side, in common with Baptists. My friend wondering at this, I observed, that Pædobaptists as well as Baptists held adult baptism; and as these passages only prove adult baptism, they prove nothing more than what is held by both. When I had made the matter sufficiently plain, our conversation

on this subject ended. He, however, called on me the next day, and said, "I am really surprised at what you said yesterday, and could hardly sleep for thinking of it."

The error I am guarding against, is that of claiming an exclusive right to those Scriptures, which do not exclusively belong to them. It is by means of this common error, that the Baptist cause is maintained; for it gives it the appearance of strength, when in reality it has none. Mr. Booth shall come forward as an example, since he is as deeply tinctured with this error as any of his brethren. In vol. ii. p. 415, he says, "That Baptists have no need of subterfuge to evade the force of any argument formed upon it, [1 Cor. vii. 14,] is plain, I humbly conceive, from the preceding reflections. No, while they have both precept and example on their side," &c.—Both precept and example on their side! This looks very formidable indeed: but let us examine the phrase. Pray, Mr. Booth, what do you mean by the Baptists' side? Do you mean adult baptism? If you mean this, it is only passing a deception upon the reader; for you must know that Pædobaptists have no dispute with you upon that subject. You certainly know that they both hold and practise adult baptism as well as you, and that what you call your side is no more yours than it is theirs. But do you mean the denial of infant baptism? This you should mean, when you distinguish your side from theirs; for herein it is, that you and Pædobaptists take different sides, seeing they affirm, and you deny, that infants are fit subjects of baptism. If so, then you affirm that Baptists have both precept and example for the denial of infant baptism, which is indeed properly your side. No, sir, very far from it; you have neither precept nor example, on your side, in all the word of God. You have nothing in the world on your side, as you are pleased to call it, but two poor sophisms, *i. e.* a pair of bad, very bad arguments, which I have placed together in one column.

But the truth is, when you speak in so lofty a tone of the Baptists' side, as having both precept and example, you only mean that adult baptism has these. Pray, sir, do you and Pædobaptists take opposite sides on the article of adult baptism? If not, why is it your side so peculiarly? You have said in this quotation, that the Baptists have no need of subterfuge. Good sir, what is a subterfuge? Is it an evasion—a deception? Why do you call that your side exclusively, which is no more your side than it is the side of the Pædobaptists? Was it because your own real side, the denial of infant baptism, was weak? And did you wish by a dexterous shift, to make it pass for strong? Pray, Mr. Booth, is not this a subterfuge? It is very extraordinary that you should fly to a subterfuge, and in that very place too, where you say the Baptists do not need any. And whereas most disputants make use of subterfuges only when they actually need them, it is extraordinary that you should make use of a subterfuge, when, as you yourself say, there is in reality no need of any such thing.

By this the reader may perceive how necessary it is to keep these things clear in his own mind, if he wishes to form a judgment on this subject according to truth; for though the Baptist side has in reality no strength at all, yet it acquires the appearance of it from the misrepresentation which I have endeavoured to expose. I have, therefore, been the more desirous of placing this matter in a fair light, because, though frequently called to speak on the subject, I was not for some years aware of the deception. Let the reader keep in view those Scriptures at the top of the scheme, which weigh equally on both sides, while I pass to the two columns, where the arguments of both are placed in opposition to each other; and by comparing these, we shall see which is the stronger, and, therefore, which is the true side of the question.

2. If the reader will turn to the scheme, he will see, on the left column, what is the real strength of the Baptist side, and what arguments they produce against the baptism of infants. I have there set down two arguments which are urged by Baptists: the one taken from a want of express precept or example to baptize infants; the other from their want of capacity to believe and repent, &c. These two are the only arguments they can produce; and if they are not good, they have nothing good to urge. With respect to the

first, that there is no express command or example for baptizing infants, the same is true respecting female communion; and so this argument, if it were good, would have a double effect: it would exclude infants from baptism, and females from the Lord's supper. And then the Baptists would be right in refusing to baptize infants; but, at the same time, they would be wrong in admitting females to the Lord's supper; but, on the contrary, if women have a right to the Lord's table, though there be no express law or example for their admission, then the argument is good for nothing. I shall say more upon this, when I come to examine Mr. Booth's defence of female communion.

As to the other argument, I mean that taken from the incapacity of infants to believe and repent, it is nothing more than a sophism. I have discovered its fallacy by applying it to different cases; and in the same way that it proved against infant baptism, it would have proved against infant circumcision—against the baptism of Christ—against the temporal subsistence of infants—and, lastly, against their eternal salvation. I have likewise shown wherein its fallacy consisted, viz. in bringing more into the conclusion than was in the premises· all this the reader may observe by recurring to the place where it is examined. The consequence is that the Baptists have nothing to place against infant baptism, but two unsound, sophistical, deceitful arguments. This is the sum total of the Baptist side; but if any Baptist think he is able either to maintain these two arguments, or to produce any thing better, I seriously invite him to the task.

3. On the opposite column I have placed the arguments for infant baptism. Their order is the most simple, and the whole consists of three parts: 1. That God formed a church on earth, and constituted infants members of that church:—2. That the membership of infants, from that time to this, has never been set aside by any order of God; consequently it still remains:—3. That as infants have a divine right to membership, they must be received as members; and as they must not be received without being baptized, they must be baptized in order to be received.

These are the arguments in one column, which are to be compared with those two on the Baptist side in the other; and by comparing them together, the reader may see on which side the evidence preponderates, and consequently on which side the truth actually lies. There are three parts on the right column, which link into each other, and form a strong chain of evidence, to be placed in opposition to two false sophistical arguments, which constitute the whole force on the Baptist side; that is, there is something to be placed against nothing—substantial evidence against a pair of sophisms: and this is to be done, that the reader may see which has the stronger side, and which the true. As far as concerns myself, I only say, I have, after many supplications for the best teaching, examined, compared, and decided, and am well satisfied with the decision: the reader, if he be a man fearing God, will go and do likewise. So much for the comparison; a few words on the evidence, by itself, will finish this part of the business.

The nature of this proof, on the side of infants, is such, that Baptists can only attack it in one part. If I affirm, as in the first part, that God did constitute infants members of his church, the Baptists grant they were once church members. If I affirm, as in the third, that every one who has a right to be a church member, has a right to be baptized, they are compelled to grant that too. So there remains but one point on which a Baptist can form an attack, and that is the second part, wherein I say, that the church-membership of infants having been once an institution of God, was never set aside either by God immediately, or by any man acting under the authority of God. This is the point then that decides the question. I will spend a few words in vindicating this turning point against the *argumentum ad hominem* made use of by Mr. Booth.

In support of this I have argued from five topics: God's method of acting in bringing the Gentiles into a church state; there never was a law of God to set their membership aside; the Jews, in Christ's time, had no apprehension of any such thing; Christ spok of infants as actually belonging to the church, and his apostle placed them in the same relation to baptism as they had been in to circumcision; and Paul, in conformity to this scheme, baptized families, particularly the jailer, and all his, straightway. Each of these is already set forth, and evinced in its proper place.

But what do the Baptists place against this evidence? Mr. Booth, in answering Dr. Williams on this subject, does neither produce one Scripture to prove that the church-membership of infants, which he grants to have existed once, was ever set aside; nor does he answer those Scriptures which the Doctor had alleged to evince the continuance of their membership. What then does Mr. Booth do? Whoever will be at the pains to read his books, will find his mode of reasoning to be of this kind. He instances a variety of things belonging to the Jewish church, such as its being national—its priesthood—its tithes—its various purifications—its holy places, holy garments, &c.; and then argues most erroneously, that as these things are done away, the membership of infants must be done away too. This, I say, is the mode of his arguing, and indeed the only argument he brings, as may be seen by any one who reads his works with care. Now this reasoning of his involves a very egregious absurdity, and a very material error in point of chronology.

I. A very egregious absurdity. Mr. Booth

seems to consider the various rites, &c. of the Jewish church as being so incorporated and interwoven with the members of that church, that the rites and they become essentially the same; and then, if the rites be taken away, he fancies that the very essence of the church is so destroyed or altered, that infant membership is gone of course. Let any one weigh Mr. Booth's reasoning in vol. ii. p. 37, and understand him on any other than this absurd principle if he can. "An apostle," says he, "has taught us, that the ancient priesthood being changed, there is made of necessity a change also in the law. That is, as Dr. Owen explains it, the whole law of commandments contained in ordinances, or the whole law of Moses, so far as it was a rule of worship and obedience unto the church; for that law it is, that followeth the fates of the priesthood." Very well. That law was changed, which was a rule of worship and obedience to the church; but what has this to do with changing the church? Is a church changed, because the rule, which directed its worship, is changed? I wonder much why Dr. Owen is here introduced, unless it be to pass off an absurdity under the sanction of a great name; as nothing can be more contrary to what Mr. Booth is going to say, than this quotation from the Doctor.

Now see Mr. Booth's curious reasoning. "We may therefore adopt the sacred writer's principle of reasoning, and say, the constitution of the visible church being manifestly and essentially altered, the law, relating to qualifications for communion in it, must of necessity be changed. Consequently, no valid inference can be drawn from the membership of infants, under the former dispensation, to a similarity of external privilege under the new covenant." Now in what way could the constitution of the church be essentially altered by a change in the law of ordinances, unless upon that absurd idea, that the ordinances and members were so compounded and incorporated with each other, as to form, in this incorporated state, the very essence of the church?

One thing we may remark in this quotation, which is, that Mr. Booth grants infants to have been church members under the former dispensation. This is granting my first argument for infant baptism; there is only one more to be maintained, *viz.* That the membership of infants has never been annulled; and this being evinced, the opposition of a Baptist is at an end, since he cannot by any means deny the conclusion. And now the whole debate is brought into this narrow limit—Has the church membership of infants at any time been set aside, or has it not? I have advanced five arguments to prove it never has been set aside. Mr. Booth says it has. If you ask him to prove it, he tells you, "the constitution of the visible church is manifestly and essentially altered." If you ask him how he proves this essential alteration? he tells you, that tithes, and purifications, and priesthood, and other things of this kind belonging to the Mosaic code, are changed or taken away; and then most absurdly infers, that infant membership is taken away too: as if a member of a church and a Mosaic rite had been the same; as if infant membership, which was long before Moses, had been nothing more than a Mosaic rite. But let us observe how grandly he reasons down infant membership.

"We may therefore," says he, "adopt the sacred writer's principle of reasoning, and say."—I have been at some pains to inform myself respecting this sentence—whether Mr. Booth meant to imitate the apostle's phraseology, or to reason after the same method, or to reason from the apostle's datum or principle, *viz.* "the priesthood being changed." I was at length inclined to view the latter as his meaning; because it seemed too trivial to tell the reader in that pompous way, "We may adopt the sacred writer's principle of reasoning," when nothing more was meant but imitation of phraseology. For the same reason I thought he could not mean an imitation of the apostle's method; for that would be only saying, he should lay down a datum as the apostle had done, and then draw an inference as the apostle did. All this is very well, and *secundum artem;* but then he might as well have told the reader, that he would adopt Aristotle's principle of reasoning, as the sacred writer's. For if Mr. Booth only meant that he would lay down a datum or principle to begin with, and then proceed to infer, it can signify nothing to any man living, unless his datum be a true one. And if this be all, he need not have introduced it with such pomp as the "sacred writer's principle of reasoning;" for what other would any person adopt, unless he were an idiot? This, as well as the other, being too trifling to be Mr. Booth's meaning, I therefore concluded he meant to adopt the apostle's datum, *viz* " The priesthood being changed," and from thence to draw an inference against infants. I was the more inclined to think he intended this, since he had just cited the apostle's words, and Dr. Owen's explanation of them; and this being done, he immediately proceeds to adopt.

The apostle does indeed say, " The priesthood being changed, there is made of necessity a change also of the law." The priesthood implied servants of the church to minister in holy things; the law was a commandment contained in ordinances, and was, as Dr. Owen said, a rule of worship and obedience to the church. The priests who were to minister, and the law, which was to regulate, were both changed: the law was changed in consequence of a change in the priesthood. Well, and what then? Why, according to Mr. Booth the argument will run thus: the priests were changed, and the rule of worship was changed, therefore the church was essentially altered, therefore infants were excluded. Is not this a good inference, The priests were changed, therefore infants were excommunicated? It might have been so, if the priests had all been infants; but even then it would only have concluded against infant priests. Every argument Mr. Booth has brought against the continuance of infant church-membership is of the same kind— tithes, purifications, holy places, &c. and of these the reader may take which he pleases, and infer accordingly. Tithes are abrogated, therefore infants are excluded. Purifications are set aside, therefore infants are shut out. Holy places, &c. are no more, therefore —not so fast—If Mr. Booth is to make good his conclusion against the perpetuity of infant membership from that datum of the apostle, "the priesthood being changed," let him have the liberty of wording his own argument—I have no objection to this—let him proceed.

"The constitution of the visible church being essentially altered"—Stop—pray, sir, is this the apostle's principle of reasoning? Do you, by that sentence, mean the same as is expressed by the apostle, "The priesthood being changed?" If you do, I will not contend for a word.—Proceed—"The constitution of the visible church [that is, the priesthood] being essentially altered or changed, the law, relating to qualifications for communion in it, [that is, in the priesthood] must of necessity be changed: consequently [because the priesthood is changed] no valid inference can be drawn from the membership of infants [that is, in the priesthood] under the former dispensation, to a similarity of external privilege under the new covenant." *Bene conclusum est a dato scriptoris sacri!* And an excellent argument it is against all those who mean to bring up their infants to be Jewish priests.

Ah, aliquis error latet! Mr. Booth did not mean to conclude so: he is disputing against infant baptism, and not against infant priesthood. Very well; but then he must have a very different datum. He is certainly at liberty to dispute and conclude as he pleases, only let him do it fairly. I certainly supposed he was reasoning from the sacred writer's principle—" The priesthood being changed;" he had just quoted it, and set Dr. Owen to explain it, and said, " We may adopt it:" But that principle, as to infants, only concludes against an infant priesthood, which was not the thing he intended.

Priests, we said, were servants to minister to the church in holy things; and if so, there is a wide difference between the priesthood being changed, and the constitution of the visible church (namely, the members who constitute it) being essentially altered. The same may be said of all the instances mentioned by Mr. Booth; these might all be changed or abrogated, and yet no essential alteration take place in the church, that is, in the members of it. I am very suspicious that Mr. Booth to make out a better conclusion, meant to pass it upon the reader, that the apostle's ex pression, "*the priesthood being changed,*" and *that* of his, "*the constitution of the visible church being essentially altered,*" were of the same import, and conveyed precisely the same idea. If this was really his design, it is not much to his honour; it must proceed from a greater love to hypothesis than to truth, or, as I rather think, it arose from that absurd idea which he seems to entertain— that the priesthood, rites, and ordinances, which were given to the church, were essentially the same with that church to which they were given. And it is on this absurd principle that his opposition to the continuance of infant membership is carried on : he turns the priesthood into a church, and every institution into an infant, and then contemplates the change of the one, and the removal of the other. In the change of priesthood he sees nothing but an essential change in the church, and fancies the removal of institutions to be the removal of infants. And now he will adopt the principle of the sacred writer :— the priesthood is changed, therefore the church is essentially altered ; this institution is taken away, there goes an infant ; that institution is abrogated, there goes another infant ; and now all the institutions are gone, and now all the infants are gone ; and then, says he, " no valid inference can be drawn from the membership of infants under the former dispensation, to a similarity of external privilege under the new covenant."—We will now leave Mr. Booth in possession of his absurdity, and take notice of,

II. A very material error in point of chronology. With respect to chronology, most persons know, that from the time of Abraham to that of instituting the priesthood, the Mosaic rites, &c. we may reckon about four hundred years. During this space of time, the church, in which infants were members, was not national; it had no levitical priesthood, there was no institution of tithes, nor was the Mosiac code of rites yet formed. All we know of the church is, that its members consisted of adults and infants, who were initiated by the same rite; that sacrifices were offered; and, it is probable, that the father of the family, or some respectable person, did officiate in their assemblies as a priest. Here is a congregational church, a simple worship, and some creditable officiating priest.

If we carry our views forward, we shall see that church, which at first was congregational, become a national church; the worship that was once simple, under the direction of the Mosiac code; and instead of a priest chosen by the people, a regular priesthood is ordained of God. Now, whether we view the congregational or national form, the simple or complex worship, the irregular or regular priesthood, we see no alteration in the constitution of the church, much less an essential one, as it respected the members of which it was composed. If therefore, the passing from congregational to national, from a simple to a complex worship, from an irregular to a regular priesthood, produced no essential alteration in the church members, then should all this be reversed, should there be a change from national to congregational, from a complex to a simple worship, from a regular to an irregular priesthood, every man in his senses must see that this can no more alter the essence of the church, than the other did.

All this is plain enough to any man except Mr. Booth; for, according to his mode of reasoning, there must have been, from the beginning, I know not how many essential alterations in the constitution of the visible church: for if, as he will have it, a change of priesthood made one essential change, then the institution of the same priesthood must have made another—so there were two changes. And, not to say any thing of the changes from Adam to Abraham, what became of the essence of the church when the functions of this priesthood, during the captivity, were suspended? For if the changing of priesthood did essentially alter the church, the institution of priesthood must have done the same; and then its suspension during the captivity, and its restoration at the close of it, must have made two more; because, according to Mr. Booth's view of things, a change of priesthood essentially alters the church.

I observe that Mr. Booth in opposing the continuance of infant membership, takes care not to go too far back; the period of Mosaic rites suits him best, and there he fixes; for this era, as he supposes, furnishes him with weapons which he does not sparingly use, especially against a dissenting minister. Here he finds not only infant membership, but a national church, a priesthood, tithes, and institutions of various kinds. Now, says Mr. Booth when reasoning with a dissenting minister, "If you will plead for the continuance of infant membership, which I grant to have existed, you must also admit a national church; you must call yourself a priest, and wear holy garments, and turn your communion-table into an altar, and demand tithes, and call your meeting a holy place." But why all this? Because, says he, all these things belonged to the same dispensation as infant membership did; and so, if you take one, you must even take all, and then you will have a tolerable body of Judaism.

Now, before we rob Mr. Booth of this miserable weapon, I would just observe, that this argument of his, which is the only one he has got, is what is called *argumentum ad hominem;* and, though often used, it is one of the weakest that can be adopted. It is calculated to make an impression on some men, whose sentiments may be of a peculiar cast; but if the same be turned against others who are of a different sentiment, it is of no force at all:—*e. g.* Mr. Booth's argument has the appearance of strength, if used against a dissenting minister; because he may reject the idea of a national church, priesthood, the right of tithes, &c.; but if the same be urged against a clergyman of the establishment who admits these, all its force is gone—it is even good for nothing. This argument derives all its force from the sentiments of the person against whom it is used; it may be very strong against one man, and very weak against another; it will serve to support error as well as truth; and, therefore, when it is a solitary argument, no dependence whatever can be placed upon it. I do not mean to discard the use of it in all cases—I grant it may answer a good purpose, if prudently managed; but this I say, it should never be a man's only argument; for that man's cause must be miserably poor indeed, which depends on one solitary argument, that will either protect truth or falsehood. Just such is the case of Mr. Booth in opposing the continuance of infant membership; and I wish him to consider seriously, whether such kind of reasoning is fit to stand against a plan of God.

Now, weak as this argument is in itself, there is one thing in Mr. Booth's case, which makes it still worse; he is indebted for the use of it to a very capital absurdity. As he is not able to prove an essential alteration in the constitution of the church, he supposes, or seems to suppose, that members and religious institutions do belong to, and equally constitute the essence of the church of God; for what else but such an absurd idea could induce him to affirm, that the church was essentially altered, and so infants cut off, merely because the institutions of the church were abrogated? Now, though this argument of his is so exceedingly weak, and the principle on which it is built so very absurd, that no one need be under any apprehension, should it remain quietly in his possession, I mean, notwithstanding, to take the liberty of changing his place, and fixing him in that station, where he shall feel himself totally deprived of its assistance.

Mr. Booth must certainly know that the national form of the church, the institution of priesthood, tithes, and other Mosaic ordinances, were of a much later date than infant church-membership. I take the liberty, therefore, of changing Mr. Booth's standing, and putting him as far back as the patriarchal age, the times of Abraham, Isaac, and Jacob. And now having placed Mr. Booth among the patriarchs, I wish him to take a view of their ecclesiastical affairs, and to indulge me at the same time with a little free conversation on that subject.

Now, sir, what do you perceive in this age of the church? Here you see the venerable patriarchs, obedient to the divine order, admitting infants to church-membership. But on the other hand, you see here no national church, no instituted priesthood, no law of tithes, nor indeed any Mosaic rites. Your favourite argument against the continuance of infant membership, derived from a national church, the levitical priesthood, tithes,

&c. is, by falling back about the space of three hundred years, fairly and irrecoverably lost. You had formed so close a connection between infant membership, a national church, a priesthood, tithes, and Mosaic rites; as if they all rose into existence at the same time, and were all to expire together. But here they stand entirely apart; infant membership is in no alliance with a national church, is totally unconnected with levitical priesthood, and has nothing at all to do with Mosaic institutions. The close union you fancied existed between these does here vanish away. And now, sir, what will you do with a dissenting minister in this case? Your *argumentum ad hominem*, the only argument you had, is lost.

Lost, did I say?—Nay, now I think of it, it is not lost neither. Oh no! so far from it, that I believe I can put you in a way whereby you may manage your matters to far greater advantage. For though, by putting you back to the patriarchal age, I deprive you of those topics with which you have been able to combat a dissenting minister, *viz.* a national church, an instituted priesthood, Mosaic rites, &c.; yet all is not lost: you will here find topics, which, if managed with dexterity, will make no inconsiderable impression on a clergyman of the establishment. You observe sir, that infant membership has nothing to do with a national church, priesthood, tithes, &c.; and then, should any clergyman of the establishment rise to defend the continuance of in fant membership, you may say to him, My good sir, if you insist upon infant church-membership now, which I myself grant to have existed in the times of Abraham, Isaac and Jacob; pray observe the consequence; you must relinquish the idea of a national church, you must cease to call yourself a priest, you must lay aside your holy garments, and finally, you must give up all your tithes. For, if you will be a patriarchal professor in infant membership, you must be so in every thing else. If you will conform to the patriarchs in one particular; in the name of consistency and common honesty, I ask, why are you not a conformist in every particular?

You see, Mr. Booth, that this is *argumentum ad hominem* against a clergyman of the establishment with a witness, and will make him feel according to its importance; for certainly it will bring him into as great a difficulty as your other argument of the same kind brought Dr. Williams. Well, what a happy invention! Here is an expedient, by which you will be able to annoy on either hand. Before, when you fixed your station among the Mosaic rites, you could only act with advantage against a non-conformist; but now, if you only step back three hundred years, you may employ your artillery as successfully against an antagonist in the establishment. And thus by stepping backward or forward, according to the cast of your adversary, which is a thing easily done, you will have it in your power to urge something against all comers. This is one of the best inventions in the world for your cause; for as you stand forth as a great disputant against infant membership, it is probable you will meet with antagonists of all kinds. This expedient—like the two edges of a sword, or the two horns of a dilemma—will enable you to meet an adversary at all points. Should you attack a dissenting minister, be sure you fix upon Mosaic rites; but if a clergyman of the establishment should prove an antagonist, you know your cue; quit that station, and fall back to the patriarchal age; and so, by humouring the business, you will be a match for both. Excuse my officiousness in suggesting any thing, especially to you, who are so well versed in all the turns of disputation; I only do it, because this thought seemed to escape you.

Candid reader, I have now done with this part of the subject, and have only to say, that of all the miserable oppositions that were ever set up against an ordinance of God, I mean infant membership in its perpetuity, I think there never was a more miserable opposition than this. The Baptists grant infant church-membership to have existed once. I have affirmed that it still exists; and this being proved, the opposition of a Baptist is at an end. I have argued from five different topics, in proof of the perpetuity of infant membership. Mr. Booth who denies this, urges against it one solitary argument; and that even the weakest of all arguments, the *argumentum ad hominem;* and this same solitary, weak argument, is founded on a gross absurdity; and finally, by removing Mr. Booth from the Mosaic rites to the patriarchal age, this solitary, absurd argument, vanishes like a ghost, and utterly forsakes him.

A SHORT METHOD

WITH THE BAPTISTS.

It is a certain fact, that when any sentiment is false, it will appear the more glaringly so, the more it is examined, and the farther it is drawn out. I have been very attentive to the tendency of Mr. Booth's reasoning, and have pledged myself more than once to take some notice of it. When a writer does not wish to be prolix in answering a large work, it is best, if he think the work erroneous, to pitch upon some prominent parts, in which the fallacy of the author is sufficiently palpable to run down and ruin his whole system. I will adopt this method with Mr. Booth's performance, wherein he expresses the sentiments, and pursues the reasoning of the Baptists in general. It is his second edition of Pædobaptism Examined, to which my attention will be chiefly directed, as that subject on which I shall more directly animadvert, is not handled in the answer to Dr. Williams; the Doctor, in his piece, having urged nothing upon it: and indeed it does not signify which of Mr. Booth's books is quoted, so far as I shall notice him.

The sentiment of the Baptists, respecting a fit subject of the baptismal ordinance, divides itself into two parts: they affirm that believing adults are fit subjects of baptism;—they deny that baptism should be administered to infants. When supporting what they affirm, the subject runs very smoothly; and no man that I know, except perhaps a Quaker, will deny the conclusion. For my own part, I am as well persuaded that a believing adult is a fit subject for baptism, as ever I was in my life; and I neither have, nor mean to say, one word against it. This is the common sentiment of Baptists and Pædobaptists, and is not, as Mr. Booth falsely and boastingly calls it, the Baptists' side. As far, therefore, as the proof of adult baptism goes, it is all very well, and exceedingly plain from Scripture, and is admitted, without dispute, by both parties.

But when the Baptists are brought to answer for their negative part, *viz.* infants are not to be baptized, their difficulties instantly commence, and the mode they adopt of conducting the debate, drives them into such extremities, as ruin the cause they mean to carry, *e. g.* Is an infant to be baptized? No says a Baptist. Why? Because baptism, says he, being a positive ordinance, no one can be deemed a proper subject of it, but by virtue of some plain, express command of God. This idea of express command, they raise so excessively high, that, sure enough, they have done the business of infants in cutting them off from baptism; but, at the same time, and by the same process, a breach is made in female communion, and women are cut off from the Lord's table. This is the first thing that rises out of their system, and which will co-operate with others to ruin it. I undertake to prove, that, according to the principles and reasonings of the Baptists, a woman, however qualified, can have no right at all to the Lord's supper.

Again, the Baptists, in order to patch their system, and give it the appearance of consistency, are under the necessity of maintaining the right of females to the Lord's table, upon the same principle on which they oppose infant baptism; but when they set about this, they make a shift to lose their principle, are transformed into Pædobaptists, reason by analogy and inference, and fall into prevarication and self-contradiction, the most miserable. This is the second thing. I, therefore, undertake to show, that the Baptists, in proving against infants, and in defending female communion, do shift their ground, contradict themselves, and prevaricate most pitifully.

Further, when an argument is urged against the Baptists from the membership of infants in the ancient church, and their being, all infants as they were, the subjects of a religious rite, the Baptists do not deny the fact of their membership; but, in order to evade the consequence, they lay violent hands on the church, the membership, and the instituted religious rite, and in this way they endeavour to effect their escape. This is the third thing. I, therefore, undertake to prove, that, according to their principles and reasonings, the ever-blessed God had no church in this world for at least fifteen hundred years.

There is another thing I thought of introducing against the Baptists in this way; but as I know not how they will answer it, (since Mr. Booth has said nothing about it, though it was in a work which he himself has noticed) I intend now to put it in another part, in the form of a query, which I shall submit to any Baptist who may think proper to write on the subject.

Here are, therefore, three things that arise out of the Baptist system, and which, if fairly evinced, are sufficient to ruin that system out of which they arise.

1. That, according to the principles and reasoning of the Baptists, a woman, however qualified, can have no right at all to the Lord's table.

2. That the Baptists, in opposing infant baptism, and defending female communion, do shift their ground, contradict themselves, and prevaricate most pitifully.

3. That according to their principles and mode of reasoning, God had no church in this world for at least fifteen hundred years.

These things I undertake to make out from the works of that venerable champion on the Baptist side, the Rev. Abraham Booth.

I will begin with the first of these, *viz.* That, according to the princip.es, &c. of the Baptists, no woman, however qualified, can have any right to the Lord's table. But before I proceed to the proof, it will be necessary to observe to the reader, that baptism and the Lord's supper are both considered by Mr. Booth as positive ordinances, which I will not dispute with him, but do grant them to be such. The reader, therefore, will remark, that as Mr. Booth's reasoning, by which he opposes infant baptism, is founded upon this, that baptism is a positive institution; the same reasoning is also applicable to the Lord's supper, because that is likewise a positive rite. This Mr. Booth will not deny, nor can he deny it, without overturning his own system. Then, as the institutions are both positive, and the same reasoning will apply to both, I undertake to prove,

1. That, according to the principles and reasonings of the Baptists, a woman, however qualified, can have no right at all to the Lord's supper.

That I may make this matter as plain as possible to the reader, it will be needful to set down various topics from which female right to the Lord's supper may be, or is at any time evinced. I say then, if women have a right to the Lord's table, that right must be proved from some or all of the following considerations: *viz.* From their being in the favour of God—from their fitness for such an ordinance, as godly persons—from the benefit it may be to them—from their church-membership—from their baptism—or, lastly, from some express precept or example in the word of God. Let us form each of these into a question.

Question 1. Can the right of a woman to the Lord's table be proved from their interest in God's favour?

Answer. Mr. Booth says, No.—Vol. ii. p. 227. " But supposing it were clearly evinced that all the children of believers are interested in the covenant of grace, it would not certainly follow that they are entitled to baptism. For baptism, being a branch of positive worship, [and so the Lord's supper] depends *entirely* on the sovereign will of its Author, which will, revealed in positive precepts, or by apostolic examples, is the *only rule* of its administration."—" So far is it from being a fact, that an interest in the new covenant, and a title to positive institutions [baptism and the Lord's supper] may be inferred the one from the other." Page 228. " All reasoning from data of a moral kind, is wide of the mark."

Note. No interest in the covenant of grace, or the new covenant, however clearly evinced, can give any right to a positive institution, *i. e.* either to baptism or the Lord's supper. Then a woman, being in the covenant of grace, or in God's favour, has no right on that account to the Lord's supper; for all this depends only on positive precept or example.

Question 2. Can the right of females be proved from their suitableness to that ordinance as godly persons?

Answer. Mr. Booth affirms it cannot. Vol. i. p. 227. " But when our Divine Lord, addressing his disciples in a positive command, says, ' It shall be so ;' or, when speaking by an apostolic example, he declares, ' It is thus,' all our own reasonings about *fitness*, expediency, or utility, must hide their impertinent heads." Vol. ii. p. 228. " This being the case, we may safely conclude, that all reasoning from data of a moral kind, and the supposed fitness of things, is wide of the mark." Vol. ii. p. 389. " But were we to admit the great Vitringa's presumptions as facts, *viz*. That the infants of believing parents are sanctified by the Holy Spirit, p. 377, yet, while positive appointments are under the direction of positive laws, it would not follow that such children should be baptized."

Note. Our being sanctified, and thereby possessing a fitness for a positive institution, gives us no right at all to that institution, be it what it may. No right to any institution, according to Mr. Booth, can be inferred from sanctification of the Spirit; and all our reasoning from fitness, or supposed fitness, is altogether impertinent, and must hide its impertinent head. So no woman, Mr. Booth being judge, has a right to the Lord's table, on account of her being a sanctified or godly person.

Question 3. Can the right of females to the Lord's table be proved from the benefit or usefulness of that ordinance to them?

Answer. Mr. Booth denies that it can. Vol. i. p. 23. " Seeing baptism [and the Lord's supper too] is as really and entirely a positive institution, as any that were given to the chosen tribes, we cannot with safety infer either the mode, or the subject of it, from any thing short of a precept, or a precedent, recorded in Scripture, and relating to that very ordinance." Vol. i. p. 227. "When our divine Lord, addressing his disciples in a positive command, says, 'It shall be so,' or, when speaking by an apostolic example, he declares, 'It is thus,' all our own reasonings about fitness, expediency, or *utility*, must hide their impertinent heads."

Note. To reason from the utility or benefit of an institution, is quite an impertinent thing; so that we cannot say, the Lord's supper may be useful to females; therefore females should be admitted to the Lord's supper: for, as Mr. Booth affirms, we cannot with safety infer either mode or subject from any thing short of precept, or precedent, recorded in Scripture, and relating to the very ordinance.

Question 4. Can this right of females be proved from their church-membership?

Answer. Mr. Booth says it cannot. Vol. i. p. 22. " Nor does it appear from the records of the Old Testament, that when Jehovah appointed any branch of ritual worship, he left either the subjects of it, or the mode of administration, to be inferred by the people, from the relation in which they stood to himself, or from general moral precepts, or from any branch of moral worship." In the answer to Dr. Williams, p. 441, Mr. Booth says,

" But had our author proved that infants are born members of the visible church, it would not thence have been inferable, independent of a divine precept, or an apostolic example, that it is our duty to baptize them. For as baptism is a positive institution," &c.

Note. Mr. Booth says, we cannot infer the right of a subject to a positive ordinance from the relation he stands in to God, not even from church-membership; consequently the membership of a female gives her no right to the Lord's table.

Question 5. Can the right of females to the supper, be proved from their baptism?

Answer. No, says Mr. Booth, vol. i. p. 22. " Nor does it appear from the records of the Old Testament, that when Jehovah appointed any branch of ritual worship, he left either the subjects of it, or the mode of administration, to be inferred by the people, from the relation in which they stood to himself, or from general moral precepts, nor yet from any *other well-known positive rite.*" Page 23. " We cannot with safety infer either the mode or the subject of it, [a positive ordinance] from any thing short of a precept or a precedent recorded in Scripture, and relating to that very ordinance." This is the burden of Mr. Booth's song.

Note. Baptism is a well-known positive rite; and Mr. Booth denies that the mode or subject of one rite could be inferred from another; consequently baptism can infer no right to the Lord's supper: for, upon Mr.

Booth's word, we cannot infer either mode or subject from any thing short of precept or example relating to that very ordinance. Now, as the right of females to the Lord's table cannot, upon the principles of the Baptists, be proved from any of the preceding topics, there remains nothing to screen them from that consequence which I am now fastening upon them, but some express command or explicit example. I come in the last place, to inquire,

Question 6. Can the right of women to the Lord's table be proved from any express law or example in Holy Scripture?

Answer. Here Mr. Booth affirms;—and I deny.

It will be necessary here to give the reader a complete view of Mr. Booth's defence of female communion. This defence is very short; but, on his principles, it is the most curious, that, I think, was ever offered to the public. It is in vol. ii. pp. 73, 74, and is as follows:

"In regard to the supposed want of an explicit warrant for admitting women to the holy table, we reply by demanding: does not Paul, when he says, Let a man examine himself, and so let him eat, enjoin a reception of the sacred supper?—1. Does not the term *anthrōpos*, there used, often stand as a name of our species, without regard to sex?—2. Have we not the authority of lexicographers, and, which is incomparably more, the sanction of common sense, for understanding it thus in this passage? — 3. When the sexes are distinguished and opposed, the word for a man is not *anthrópos*, but *aneer*. This distinction is very strongly marked in that celebrated saying of Thales. The Grecian sage was thankful to fortune that he was *anthrópos*, one of the human species, and not a beast—that he was *aneer*, a man, and not a woman.—4. Besides, when the apostle delivered to the church at Corinth what he had received of the Lord, did he not deliver a command—a command to the whole church, consisting of women as well as men? When he further says, We, being many, are one bread and one body; for we are all partakers of that one bread; does he not speak of women as well as of men?—5. Again, are there any pre-requisites for the holy supper, of which women are not equally as capable as men?—6. And are not male and female one in Christ?"—This is the whole of the defence, and I confess I have been often diverted in reading it; I thought it a curiosity, as it came from the pen of Mr. Booth, who is so great an enemy to all inference and analogy respecting positive institutions!

The whole of this defence I have divided into six parts, and these, for the sake of greater plainness, are distinguished by strokes and figures. Mr. Booth in these six parts, aims at three distinct arguments; the first is taken from the word *anthrópos*, man, which includes the three first parts; the second is taken from Paul's address to the church as a body, and takes in the fourth part; the third is from the condition and qualification of females, and comprehends the two last parts.

Since Mr. Booth offers this defence to the public as proving an explicit warrant for female communion; we must, therefore, first of all, lay down the precise idea of the term explicit. Explicit denotes that which is direct, open, and plain; and which immediately strikes the mind without reasoning upon it; *e. g.* Acts viii. 12, "They were baptized, both men and women." Here the reader instantly discerns both sexes, without inferring from any other place. And hence the term explicit is opposed to implication, *i. e.* any thing included under a general word. And it is likewise opposed to inference, *i. e.* proof drawn from some other place. An explicit warrant, therefore, is such as strikes at once; and precludes the necessity of implication, reasoning, or inferring from some other topic. Such a warrant Mr. Booth insists upon for infant baptism; and this brings him under the necessity of producing the same for female communion. Which if he be unable to do, all he has said against infants will literally stand for nothing, and his books on that subject will be even worse than waste-paper.—Now for the explicit warrant for female communion.

1. We begin with the argument from the word *anthrópos*, man, concerning which Mr. Booth says three things to evince an explicit warrant. And first, Does not the term *anthrópos*, man, often stand as a name of our

species without regard to sex? What a lame set-out towards an explicit warrant! OFTEN stand as a name of our species! That's admirable on our side! This is what the learned call presumptive evidence, and this is what Mr. Booth produces towards an explicit warrant. Does he think presumptive and explicit are the same? Whatever advantage Mr. Booth may wish to take, yet I would not grant this, were I in his place, lest some Pædobaptist should take an advantage of it too. This presumptive mode of arguing on a positive institution will not do Mr. Booth much credit; he must certainly put on a better appearance than this.

Well then, in the second place; " Have we not," says Mr. Booth, " the authority of lexicographers, and, which is incomparably more, the sanction of common sense, for understanding it thus in that passage?" 1 Cor. xi. 28. The authority of lexicographers! and common sense! Here is help for the learned, and the unlearned, that both may be able, after consultation had, to pick out an explicit warrant! For my own part, I do not much like the labour of turning over lexicographers at the best of times, and especially for an explicit warrant; *i. e.* a warrant that strikes the mind at once. I rather think Mr. Booth if he wished people to labour for that which should be had without any labour at all, should have sent his inquirers to commentators as well as to lexicographers, to know how the apostle used the word in question. But suppose we depend on the authority of these lexicographers, it may still be proper to ask, how it is they know in what manner the apostle used this word! Do they know by analogy, or by inferring from other premises? Ah! Mr. Booth! I fear these gentry would betray you. And to give you your due, you do not seem to place much confidence in them; for you say, that the authority of common sense is incomparably more.

Common sense! Hardly one in five hundred is able to consult a lexicographer, and therefore Mr. Booth in order to make his explicit warrant explicit, furnishes help to the unlearned. Well, common sense! since it pleases Mr. Booth, though you do not understand Greek, to submit to your determination, whether *anthrópos* be an explicit word for a woman, and so, whether there be any explicit warrant for female communion, I will take the liberty of asking a few questions. Do you know what Mr. Booth means to prove from 1 Cor. xi. 28. Let a man, *anthrópos*, examine himself, &c.? Yes, he means to prove an explicit warrant for female communion. Very well. What is an explicit warrant? It is that, the sense of which you instantly perceive, without the necessity of reasoning upon it, or inferring it from some other part. Can a warrant be deemed explicit, if it be not founded on explicit words? Certainly not; for the words constitute the warrant. If the word *anthrópos*, man, be used sometimes for a male infant of eight days old, John vii. 22, 23; and perhaps a hundred times in the New Testament for a male adult only; and nineteen times in the Septuagint and New Testament, to distinguish the male from the female, when both are named; would you, after all this, consider it as an explicit word for a woman? No, it is impossible. Mr. Booth says, he has your authority for understanding it as a name of our species, *i. e.* comprehending male and female, in this place; but if this word be not an explicit word for a woman, how do you know that women as well as men are included in it? I conclude it from this, that women as well as men were baptized; that they were received into the church; and therefore must be implied in this word. You conclude it by analogy, implication, and inference! These are fine materials for an explicit warrant!

But if the authority of lexicographers and common sense will not bring the business home, Mr. Booth is determined to make use of his own authority. He has no other way of preserving the credit of his book; and, therefore, he will even risk his own reputation, rather than lose his explicit warrant. He ventures in the third part to say, that, " when the sexes are distinguished and opposed, the word for a man is not *anthropos*, but *aneer*." This is Mr. Booth's own, and he himself is accountable for it. The assertion is made use of, to give a colour to his explicit warrant; and it was, no doubt, the necessity of his case that drove him to this. He had pressed the Pædobaptists, through a great part of his eight hundred and seventy-five pages, to produce an explicit warrant for infant baptism; and having thereby forged a chain for himself, he is now entangled in his turn. It is sufficient for me in this place to say, that this assertion of Mr. Booth is unfounded. I have already presented the reader with nineteen instances out of the Septuagint and New Testament, which lie directly against him. Mr. Booth in order to pass off this assertion of his with a better grace, nas given us a quotation, though not at all to the point, from Diogenes, out of his Life of Thales. What I have to say respecting the quotation, is this, that had Diogenes, or any one else, affirmed the same as Mr. Booth (which he has not, nor Thales either,) I would have linked them together as two false witnesses. And I say further, it seems a marvellous thing, that Mr. Booth should be so well acquainted with Thales, and his biographer Diogenes; and at the same time so ignorant of his own Bible.

This is Mr. Booth's first argument to prove an explicit warrant; and the parts of which it is composed are three. It is said, indeed, "a threefold cord is not easily broken." But Solomon did not mean such a cord as Mr. Booth's; his is what people commonly call a rope of sand; which will by no means endure stretching. Here we have, in this part, a presumption to begin with; and next, implication and inference; and lastly, an unfounded declaration to close the whole. This is Mr. Booth's method of making up an explicit warrant! And every one knows, that when presumption takes the lead, it is no wonder if falsehood should bring up the rear.

2. I come now to take notice of his second argument, taken from Paul's address to the church as a body; and which takes in the fourth part of his defence of female communion. His words are these: " besides, when the apostle delivered to the church at Corinth what he had received of the Lord; did he not deliver a command—a command to the whole church, consisting of women as well as men?" When he further says, " We being many, are one bread and one body; for we are all partakers of that one bread; does he not speak of women as well as men?" This is Mr. Booth's way of producing an explicit warrant; did he not deliver a command to the whole church, consisting of women as well as men? and did he not speak of women as well as men? It was Mr. Booth's place to show by *explicit* words, that he did speak of women as well as men; but since he has only proposed his questions, and has not himself affirmed any thing, he seems willing to throw the work of inferring off from himself upon the reader. Mr. Booth is an artful disputant; he knew that reasoning by inference, which he had so often exploded, would be highly unbecoming in him; and therefore, to avoid that, he puts it into the form of a

question, as if he would say, I leave you, my reader, to draw the inference.

If by the command in this argument Mr. Booth means these words, "Let a man examine himself, &c." he had spoken upon it in his way before: and if it had contained any explicit warrant for female communion, it was certainly in his power to show it: there could, therefore, be no necessity to produce it again, and especially in the obscure manner he has done. But if that be the command he intends, I defy him to show one explicit word for female communion in any part of it. He has, indeed, in what he thought fit to advance upon it, ventured a presumption, an inference, and an unfounded declaration; of all which I have spoken sufficiently already.

But I rather think he means some other command, because he introduces it with the word "besides," as if intending some fresh matter. And if so, I know no more than the pen in my hand, what command it is he drives at. But be it what it may, he asks, whether it was not to women as well as men? And I, on the other hand, declare I neither know what it was, nor to whom it was directed. It certainly was his duty to have specified what the command was; and if it was a command to receive the Lord's supper, he should then have proved that females were as explicitly named therein as males. Does Mr. Booth think that, after all he has said about express commands, he himself is to take any thing for granted, or to form a conclusion by a guess? It must be absurd in a man like him, who, when he pretends to produce an explicit warrant, talks to his reader about some unknown command; and then, instead of specifying what this command was, and showing that women were expressly named therein, leaves him, in the best way he can, to conjecture the whole.

Mr. Booth having expressed himself plainly on the first argument, did thereby lay himself open to detection, and it became an easy business to expose him for his presumptive argument, his inference, and his assertion: but he has saved himself from that, in his second argument, merely by the obscurity of his language. Saved himself, did I say, by the obscurity of his language? No, far from it. A man renders himself sufficiently ridiculous, who comes full of his explicit warrant for female communion, and then says to his reader, Did not the Apostle deliver a command to women, as well as to men? and did he not speak to women, as well as to men? When it was his business to show that he did, and to bring explicit words to prove it.

3. I advert, lastly, to Mr. Booth's third argument, which is taken from the condition and qualification of females, and comprehends the last two parts. Thus he expresses himself: " again, are there any pre-requisites for the holy supper, of which women are

not equally capable as men? And are not male and female one in Christ?"—I have no reason to complain of the ambiguity of this argument, any more than that of the first; it is sufficiently plain, that even he that runs may read it. I shall, therefore, only briefly observe upon it, that

The mode of reasoning, which Mr. Booth has openly adopted in this place, is that of analogy. The analogy lies between the male and the female, thus: that the one has the same pre-requisites for the Lord's table as the other, and both the one and the other are in Jesus Christ. From hence arises an inference: if both have the same relation to Christ, and the same pre-requisites for the holy supper, then the female must, by just consequence, have the same right to the holy supper as the male.

Well said, Mr. Booth! This is so neat, that I could almost find in my heart to forget that explicit warrant, which you had spoken of some time ago. Now, you talk like a logical man, and a generous man too; for your last is better by far than your first. It must be much better to be thus open, than to hazard your reputation by any thing forced, or any thing false. You see what a good thing it is to have analogy and inference ready at hand, and how admirably adapted they are to help at a dead lift. We should not despise any help, as we know not how soon we may need it; and, to give you your due, you have been neither too proud nor too stub born to make use of this. You may be the more easily excused for what you have said against analogy and inference, for, as you are a Baptist, what you have said was a matter of consistency; but now you are become a patron of female communion, the case is altered, and you are altered with it. But, at the same time, this is no more than what all the Baptists, with whom I have ever conversed on the subject, have done; and if it will be any comfort to you in this case, I can tell you, with great certainty, that I have met with many of your fraternity who have been as great changelings in this business as yourself. At present I only blame you for this, that, under the colour of explicit proof, you should introduce, and endeavour to pass off, nothing better, but something far worse, than inferential reasoning.

I would just remark on what Mr. Booth has advanced in support of his explicit warrant, that the defence he has set up carries in it its own conviction. I mean with respect to the number of particulars—the manner in which they are proposed—and the matter of which they consist.

Now it is the nature of an explicit warrant to show itself instantly to the mind of the reader; and its own evidence is the strongest it can have; the consequence is that he who really produces one, neither can, nor does need, to strengthen it by any reasons he can advance *e. g.* Were I called upon to produce an explicit warrant for female baptism. I would only allege those words in Acts viii. 12. "They were baptized both men and women." These words strike the mind at once, and no reasoning whatever can add any thing to their strength or evidence; but Mr. Booth, by introducing six particulars, shows plainly that neither of them is explicit, and that it is not in his power to produce any explicit warrant at all; for had any one of these been explicit for female communion, he might very well have thrown away all the rest.

In this view there is another thing remarkable in his defence, and that is, that every sentence but one runs in the form of a question to the reader. Instead of advancing his explicit proof, Mr. Booth comes to the reader *in forma pauperis*, with his petition in his mouth, as if he would say, O generous reader, grant me what I ask, or—my cause is ruined! I have been driving against infant baptism with all my might, crying out, No explicit warrant, no explicit warrant for infant baptism in all the word of God! And now, as I am called upon myself to give an explicit warrant for female communion, I beseech thee, indulgent reader, to admit my presumption, implication, inference, and analogy, for explicit proof. I said that every sentence in this defence but one was put in the form of a question. Now what is still more remarkable is this, that that one sentence, which is the only affirmative in the whole defence, should be the very false assertion against which I have already produced nineteen instances.

If we pass from the number of parts which are contained in this defence, and the manner in which they are presented to the reader, and come to the matter of it, we may say of that, that there is not a single article in it, but what is either false, or presumptive, or inference, or analogy, or implication. Every part is reducible to one or other of these; and there is not one explicit word for female communion throughout the whole. Such a defence as this would not have done very well in the hands of a Pædobaptist; but when adopted by a Baptist, it is ridiculous in himself, and an insufferable abuse of, and a burlesque upon, his reader. In short, there is no explicit warrant to be had.

Now to the point. I was to prove that, according to the principles and reasonings of the Baptists, a woman, however qualified, can have no right at all to the Lord's supper. We have seen on the one hand, that it is not possible to produce an explicit warrant for female communion, and, on the other, Mr. Booth affirms that they should not be admitted without one; the result, therefore, is, that, according to Mr. Booth's mode of reasoning, no woman has any right at all to communicate at the Lord's table; and as Mr. Booth agrees with Baptists in general in this point, the same is true of the principles and reasonings of them all.—This is the first consequence which I undertook to make good among the

Baptists, and from which they have only two ways of clearing themselves. They must either give up their mode of reasoning against infants, or, if they do not choose this, they must produce the same express proof for female communion as they require for infant baptism.

As Mr. Booth has plainly asserted that there can be no argument for female communion but such as is founded on positive precept or example, recorded in Scripture, and relating to that very ordinance, it lies upon him to come forward and produce his warrant, or give up female communion. If I were to answer his book, I would turn the inquiry from infant baptism to female communion, and then put it upon him to make good his conclusion for the right of females upon the very same principles which he employs against infants. And I do now in good earnest put this upon him, and heartily invite him to the task, being verily persuaded that if this subject were thoroughly sifted, it would be the speediest method of adjusting the debate.

When I had compared what Mr. Booth has said against infants with what he has said in defence of women, I have been ready to suspect that he designed his book should operate on the Pædobaptist side; for, when speaking against infant baptism, he carries his demand of express, unequivocal, and explicit proof so high, and enlarges upon it so much, as if, by making it exceedingly remarkable, he wished some one to compare the whole with his defence of female communion, and perceived that the moment this was done, the cause of the Baptists would fall. And had Mr. Booth been a person whose character for integrity was not known, it would have been a matter of some difficulty with me to determine whether he did not design, in a covert way, to run down the Baptists' side. But knowing him to be a man of good reputation, I readily acquit him of this; yet I think, at the same time, that his book, though written on the Baptist side, will do more towards over turning the Baptist sentiment than any one that has been written for many centuries.

Thus much for the first consequence, viz. that, according to the reasonings of the Baptists, no woman has any more right to the Lord's supper than an infant has to baptism. But they, not liking this consequence, are induced to set up a defence of female communion on the ground of express warrant; and in doing this, they prevaricate, discard their own principle, reason by analogy and inference, and fall into self-contradiction: this is the second consequence I have before mentioned, and which I will now plainly evince.

Mr. Booth, in vol. ii. p. 509, expresses his surprise at the inconsistency of Pædobaptists with each other. " But is it not," says he, " I appeal to the reader; is it not a very singular phenomenon in the religious world, that so many denominations of protestants should all agree in one general conclusion, and yet differ to such an extreme about the premises whence it should be inferred?" To this I only say, if it be a very singular phenomenon for a number of persons to be inconsistent with each other, it must be a more singular one still for one man to differ from himself. We will take a view of Mr. Booth in a double capacity—as a patron of female communion, and as an opposer of infant baptism.

Mr. Booth's defence of female communion does not take up one clear page; the erroneous statement, and the quotation made use of to set it off, make up more than one third of the defence; so there are only nineteen lines remaining: I will, therefore, select some passages from his opposition to infant baptism, and place them against what he has advanced, in these nineteen lines, in defence of female communion. I do this to show that a Baptist cannot maintain that ground on which he opposes infant baptism—that he is compelled to desert his own principle, and does actually prevaricate, and contradict himself; from which, as well as from other topics, it will appear, that the cause of the Baptists is a lost cause. I shall now introduce Mr. Booth in his double capacity.

I. When Mr. Booth is an opposer of infant baptism, he speaketh on this wise: Vol. ii. p. 228. "This being the case, we may safely conclude that all reasoning from data of a moral kind, and the supposed fitness of things, is wide of the mark." Vol. i. p. 227. "But when our divine Lord, addressing his disciples in a positive command, says, 'It shall be so,' or when, speaking by an apostolic example, he declares, 'It is thus,' all our own reasonings about *fitness,* expediency, or utility, must hide their impertinent heads."

But when Mr. Booth becomes a defender of female communion, he expresseth himself thus: Vol. ii. pp. 73, 74. "In regard to the supposed want of an explicit warrant for admitting women to the holy table, we reply by demanding—Are there any pre-requisites for the holy supper, of which women are not equally capable as men?" Thus Mr. Booth. He only asks the question, and leaves the inference to the reader. This is artfully done, for fear he should seem to prove a right to a positive institution by inference.

The reader is desired to observe, that Mr. Booth in opposing infant baptism, will admit of no reasoning from moral data, or the supposed fitness of things, and says that all such reasoning is wide of the mark. And he likewise says, "that all our reasonings about fitness—must hide their impertinent heads." But, in defending female communion, he asks, "Are there any pre-requisites for the holy supper, of which women are not equally capable as men?" Here Mr. Booth, the patron of female communion, adopts the same reasoning which Mr. Booth, the opposer of infant baptism, had declared to be wide of the mark. As the patron of females, he will reason from the fitness of things—"are there any prerequisites for the holy supper, of which women are not equally capable as men?" As the opposer of infants, he insisted that all such reasonings should hide their impertinent heads. If the patron of females and the opposer of infants be the same person, he must be guilty of gross inconsistency; for he attempts to pass off that reasoning upon others, which he himself declares to be wide of the mark; and will needs bring those heads of reasoning to light, which he brands with the name of impertinent, and says that their impertinent heads must be hid. This in and out proceeding of the patron of females and opposer of infants I submit to the judgment of the reader, and leave the patron and opposer to settle the matter the best way he can.

II. Again, Mr. Booth when opposing infant baptism, says, vol. i. p. 23. " Seeing baptism is really and entirely a positive institution, we cannot with safety infer either the mode or the subject of it from any thing short of a precept, or a precedent, recorded in Scripture, and relating to that very ordinance." Vol. ii. p. 227. " Baptism, being a branch of positive worship, depends entirely on the sovereign will of its Author; which will, revealed in positive precepts, or by apostolic examples, is the only rule of its administration." And in vol. ii. p. 44, he says, " The inquirer has nothing to do but open the New Testament, and consult a few express commands and plain examples, and consider the natural and proper sense of the words, and then, without the aid of commentators, or the help of critical acumen, he may decide on the question before him." A little after he speaks of express commands and express examples, which is his uniform mode of expression when opposing infants.

But when Mr. Booth comes to defend female communion, he expresses himself thus: Vol. ii. p. 73. " In regard to the supposed want of an explicit warrant for admitting women to the holy table, we reply by demanding— Does not the term *anthrópos*, there used, *often* stand as a name of our species without regard to sex? Have we not the authority of lexicographers, and, which is incomparably more, the sanction of common sense, for understanding it thus in that passage? When the sexes are distinguished and opposed, the word for a man is not *anthrópos* but *aneer*."

The reader is requested to notice, that Mr. Booth, as an opposer of infant baptism, contends for precept, positive precept, express commands, or express examples, and says, in his index, that the law of institutions must be express, &c. but, as a defender of female communion, he takes up with an ambiguous word, a mere presumptive proof—" Does not," says he, " the term *anthrópos often stand* as a name of our species?" and this presumption he attempts to strengthen by an error, of which I have already spoken. As an opposer of infants he says the inquirer may decide the question without the aid of commentators, or the help of critical acumen; but as a patron of females, he first furnishes his reader with an ambiguous word, and then sends him to lexicographers to have it manufactured into a positive one. Since it was not in Mr. Booth's power to form a positive precept out of an ambiguous word, without the aid of a little inference, he very artfully throws it into the hands of lexicographers and common sense to effect this business for him. And one cannot sufficiently admire how tenacious he is of express precept when an opposer of infants, while at the same time, as the patron of females, he is so very complying, that he can even admit presumptive evidence to pass for an explicit warrant.

III. Further, Mr. Booth, in opposing infant baptism, expresses himself thus: Vol. i. p. 22, " Nor does it appear from the records of the Old Testament, that when Jehovah appointed any branch of ritual worship, he left either the subjects of it, or the mode of administration, to be inferred by the people from the relation in which they stood to himself, or from general moral precepts, or from any branch of his moral worship, nor yet from any other well-known positive rite; but he gave them special directions relating to the very case." In vol. ii. p. 227, he says, " But supposing it were clearly evinced that all the children of believers are interested in the covenant of grace, it would not certainly follow that they are entitled to baptism; for baptism being a branch of positive worship, depends entirely on the sovereign will of its Author, which will, revealed in positive precepts, or by apostolic examples, is the only rule of its administration." And in the same page he says, " So far is it from being a fact, that an interest in the new covenant, and a title to positive institutions may be inferred the one from the other."

But in proving the right of women to the Lord's table, he says, vol. ii. pp. 73, 74. In regard to the supposed want of an explicit warrant for admitting women to the holy table, we reply by demanding—Are not male and female one in Christ?" As if he should say, if a female be in Christ, which is the same as being in the covenant of grace, she must have a right to a positive institution. Here is art and inference together! The art appears in this, that Mr. Booth would not be seen to draw the inference himself, but leaves that to a Pædobaptist, who is more accustomed to that kind of work.

But leaving Mr. Booth's art in shunning to draw the inference, I would desire the reader to attend him once more in his double capacity. In that of an opposer of infants, he affirms, that a right to a positive ordinance is not to be inferred from the relation we stand in to God; when a patron of females, he will infer their right to the Lord's supper from their being one in Christ with males. As an opposer of infants, he insists that an interest in the covenant of grace, though clearly evinced, gives no claim to an instituted rite as a patron of females, he contends that if a woman be interested in Christ, she has therefore a right to such an institution. As an opposer, he declares it is far from being a fact, that an interest in the new covenant, and a title to positive institutions, may be inferred the one from the other ; as a patron, he will do that which is so far from being a fact. He infers the one from the other, the right from the interest—" are not male and female one in Christ?" He is very inflexible as an opposer, and very pliant as a patron. So that, however the opposer of infants may differ in his mode of reasoning from Pædobaptists, the patron of females finds it necessary to reason in the same way. It is a pity the patron and opposer do not agree, as it would certainly be for the credit of both to settle on some uniform mode of logic.

Before I turn from this, I would just glance at Mr. Booth's defence of female communion by itself. Mr. Booth should have made this a distinct chapter, and should have placed a title at the head of it ; but as he has not done this, I will take the liberty of doing it for him ; and the reader may observe, in the mean time, how the chapter and title will agree. Mr. Booth begins his defence in these words : " in regard to the supposed want of an explicit warrant for admitting women to the holy table, we reply," &c. This will furnish with a title, which will run thus:

The right of Women to the Lord's Table, founded on explicit warrant.

N. B. An explicit warrant for females is one wherein their sex is specified, and is opposed to all implication, analogy, and inference......Now for the Chapter.

"Does not Paul, when he says, 'Let a man examine himself and so let him eat,' enjoin a reception of the sacred supper? Does not the term *anthrópos*, there used, *often* stand as a name of our species, without regard to sex?" [This is presumptive proof.] "Have we not the authority of lexicographers, and, which is incomparably more, the sanction of common sense, for understanding it thus in that passage?" [This is inference.] "When the sexes are distinguished and opposed, the word for a man is not *anthrópos*, but *aneer.*" [This is an error.] "When the apostle delivered to the church at Corinth what he had received of the Lord, did he not deliver a command—a command to the whole church, consisting of women as well as men?" [This at best is implication or presumption.] "When he further says, We, being many, are one bread and one body, for we are all partakers of that one bread, does he not speak of women as well as of men?" [This is the same as before; and Mr. Pierce would have said, "infants," as well as men and women.] "Again, are there any pre-requisites for the holy supper of which women are not equally capable as men?" [This is analogy and inference together.] "And are not male and female one in Christ?" [This is analogy and inference again.]

The reader will observe that the Title promises an explicit warrant, that is, a warrant in which the sex is specified, and which stands opposed to implication, analogy, and inference; but the chapter produces nothing explicit, the whole being nothing more than a compound of presumption, implication, analogy, and inference.

The whole of Mr. Booth's conduct in this affair brings to mind a passage of Mr. Alsop, which Mr. Booth has quoted in vol. ii. p. 507. "The reader will learn at least how impossible it is for error to be consonant to itself. As the two mill-stones grind one another as well as the grain, and as the extreme vices oppose each other as well as the intermediate virtue that lies between them, so have all errors this fate, (and it is the best quality they are guilty of,) that they duel one another with the same heat that they oppose the truth." Mr. Booth's two mill-stones are his opposition to infant baptism, and his defence of female communion. These two militant parts, like the two mill-stones, do operate in hostile mode, and rub, and chafe, and grind each other, as well as infant baptism, which lies between. And it is certainly the best property Mr. Booth's book is possessed of, that it exhibits the author in his double capacity, not only as militating against the baptism of infants, but as duelling and battering himself

with the same heat with which he opposes
that. Three short reflections on this conduct
of Mr. Booth and one apology will finish this
part of the subject.

I. There is something in this conduct very
unfair. No man should bind a burden on
others, which he himself would not touch
with one of his fingers. Can it be deemed
an upright proceeding in Mr. Booth to cry
down all reasoning by analogy and inference on
a positive institution, and after that use the
same reasoning, and even worse, himself? Can
it be considered fair to demand, repeatedly
and loudly to demand, special, express, and
explicit proof, and then put off the reader
with presumption, inference, and analogy?
Certainly he should do as he would be done
by; but if this conduct of his be fair, I know
not what is otherwise.

II. There is something in this conduct
very impolitic. After Mr. Booth had demanded
positive, express, and explicit proof, and had
run down all proof by analogy and inference, he should, if he had had but a little
policy, have kept that defence of female
communion entirely out of sight. It was
not crafty in him, though there is a spice of
it in the defence itself, to suffer that to go
abroad, which, when set against what he
had said in opposition to infant baptism,
would run down and ruin the whole. Had
I been he, and wished my other arguments
to stand, I would have taken that defence,
and thrown it into the fire.

III. There is something in this conduct very unfortunate It is a sad case that a book should be so written, that one part shall rise up against and ruin the other. Mr. Booth, Samson-like, when opposing infant baptism, thinks he can carry gates and bars, and every thing else away; but when he defends female communion, Samson-like again, he becomes like another man, that is, a Pædobaptist; for he reasons, infers, and proves, in the very same way. In one thing, however, he differs, and herein he is unfortunate, that instead of killing the Philistines, to wit, the arguments of Pædobaptists, he falls to combating himself, and destroys his own.

What shall we say to these things? I reply, that with respect to myself I say thus much: that as he is unfair, I would reprove him; as he is impolitic, I would excuse him; as he is unfortunate, I would pity him; and, under all these views, I would make the best apology for him which the nature of the case will admit.

Since it is evident that Mr. Booth demands express, positive, and explicit proof, with respect to the mode and subject of an instituted rite, and as it is equally evident that he himself reasons on such a rite by implication, analogy, and inference, the apology I make for him, and it is the best I can make, is this: that he understood explicit proof, which he had so much insisted on, and proof by inference, which he himself adopted, to mean precisely the same thing; so that when any thing was proved by inference, &c. that proof was considered by him as express and explicit. This, I say, is the best apology I can make for those repugnancies, or, (if this apology be admitted,) seeming repugnancies, I find in his book. But, methinks, I hear some Pædobaptist say, If this apology be good, it will indeed reconcile some of his inconsistencies, but then he will, at the same time, stand in need of another; for if express proof and proof by inference be the same thing, I should be glad to know why he wrote his book at all. To this I can only say, that I have no other apology to make; let him apologize for himself. Leaving Mr. Booth or any one else, to manage these incongruities the best way he can, I pass to the third consequence, namely,

That, according to the principles and reasonings of the Baptists, God had no church in this world at least for fifteen hundred years.

The way in which the Baptists are driven into this consequence is this: when it is urged against them that infants were constituted church members, and were, by the Lord himself, deemed fit subjects of a religious rite, they, in order to avoid a consequence which would bear hard on their arguments, endeavour to reduce this church into a mere civil society; and as they cannot deny the membership of infants, they try to escape by destroying the church. Now, as this is a necessary consequence of their principle, it will serve to discover the error of that principle of which it is a consequence.

Mr. Booth, in trying to effect his escape in this way, has used a language, which, if true, will prove that God for many centuries had no church at all in this world. This is Mr. Booth's expedient, but it is a desperate one. In vol. ii. p. 252, he calls the then existing church, an " ecclesiastico-political constitution." By this compound word he seems to consider the church under the notion of an amphibious society; partly civil, and partly religious. And he might have likewise considered, that, as nothing in nature differs more than policy among men and piety towards God, they must be viewed in all bodies of men, whether large or small, as things totally and at all times distinct. But this Mr. Booth's system would not admit. Now in a large body, as the Jews for instance, all laws pertaining to human society, as such, were civil laws; and all laws, though in the same code with the others, relating to the worship of God, were; properly speaking, ecclesiastical laws. So with respect to men, when they are united in promoting order and mutual security, they are to be considered as a political state; but if some, or all of these profess piety towards God, and unite in his worship, they are to be viewed as a visible church. And though all the inhabitants of Judea belonged to the state, it will not follow that all belonged to the visible church. There were without doubt some excommunicated persons, some who voluntarily withdrew, and there might be many, who came into the land of Israel, that did not join themselves to the Lord. There was, therefore, no just reason why Mr. Booth should confound things, which in their own nature are, and ever must be, separate. Neither is it probable he would have done it, if he had not been compelled by his opposition to the continuance of infant-membership.

Though Mr. Booth, by the phrase ecclesiastico-political constitution, has confounded the church and state, the one being a kingdom of this world, the other the kingdom of Christ; yet as something of church still makes its appearance, the consequence charged on Baptist principles may not seem to be clearly evinced. 'Tis true, he seems to grant two parts, the political and ecclesiastical; but if we look more narrowly into his book, the ecclesiastical part disappears, and nothing will remain but the political only.

In vol. ii. p. 251, Mr. Booth has these emphatic words: "to be an obedient subject of their [the Jews'] civil government, and a complete member in their church-state, were the same thing." Every one knows, that a civil government, be it where it may, is conversant about present things, it is a government among [*cives*] citizens as such, and is designed to regulate their worldly concerns. An obedient subject of such a government, is one who quietly and cheerfully submits to its regulations, and seeks the peace and security of that community to which he belongs. Now Mr. Booth assures us that such was the nature of things among the Jews, that "an obedient subject of the civil government, and a complete member of the church-state, were the same." If this were so, it must be because the civil government was nothing less than the church; and the church was nothing more than the civil government; that is, they were both the same thing. It signifies nothing by what name we call this community, whether a national church, or an ecclesiastico-political constitution; it means no more at last than a civil government: for, as Mr. Booth informs us, there was nothing more required in a complete member of what he calls the church, than his being an obedient subject of the civil government. Now as this, whatever it was, could be no church of God, and as it is not supposed there was a church of a higher nature in any other part; it will follow, that, according to Mr. Booth's principles, God had for many centuries no such thing as a church, properly so called, in this world.

What a church destroyer is this same Mr. Booth! And when we consider that all this results from principle, and is carried on by regular logical process; what a horrid principle must that be which leads a man to destroy the very church of God! Though I have been a Baptist myself for several years, I never till lately discerned this shocking consequence of the Baptist sentiment. And I am much indebted to Mr. Booth for an insight into this, as well as other consequences which necessarily result from the Baptist scheme.

And I have no doubt but his book, when nicely examined, will do more good this way than any thing which has hitherto been written on the subject.

As Mr. Booth to preserve his system, has laid violent hands on the ancient church of God; we cannot suppose that that which was connected with it could possibly escape. He that could reduce the church into a civil government, will not think it much to manufacture a religious institution into a political rite. What was circumcision? According to Mr. Booth " it was a sign of carnal descent, a mark of national distinction, and a token of interest in temporal blessings." Here indeed is a good match; a civil institution, and a civil government! Now, though there is not a word of truth in all this; yet this honour Mr. Booth shall have, and it is an honour I cannot always give him, that in this he is actually consistent with himself: he has secularized the church and the institution together.

I will not now contend with Mr. Booth whether he has given a true account of the ancient church, and its members; it is sufficient for my present purpose to take notice of what he has affirmed. Yet I could wish, should he write again upon the subject (as I hope he will,) to see a fuller account of that church, the complete members of which were only obedient subjects of the civil government. I have never, in my small reading, met with a definition of a church like this; it is enough for me now that Mr. Booth has. My business is not to dispute, but to take it upon his word I only say, that if such a church did ever exist, whatever it was, it could be no church of God. And as there was no better church, *i. e.* a civil government, in any other part; there was not, on Mr. Booth's principles, for many centuries, a church of God, properly so called, in all the world.

"An obedient subject of their civil government, and a complete member of their church state, were the same thing." The same thing! If, then, the complete member was no more than an obedient subject; the church state could be no more than a civil government: for, according to Mr. Booth they were precisely the same thing. What might be the reason of all this? Mr. Booth shall inform us himself; it was, " because by treating Jehovah as their political sovereign, they avowed him as the true God." As it is not my business in this place to oppose any thing Mr. Booth says; I shall only take the liberty to explain. What is a political sovereign? He is one who reigns over others in civil things; that is, he governs and regulates the affairs of this present world. This is the reason then, that an obedient subject of civil government, and a complete church member, were the same thing; because al. that God had to do with them was, as a political sovereign, to regulate the affairs of the present world.

But where would have been the harm of supposing the ever-blessed Jehovah to have been more, infinitely more, than a political sovereign? And that he gave his word and ordinances to lead to the faith of Christ? That he sent his prophets to bear witness, that through his name whosoever believed in him should receive remission of sins? That he formed a people for himself, to show forth his praise? Where, I say, would have been the harm of supposing this? None at all, in reality; the harm would only have been to Mr. Booth's system. For had Jehovah been a religious sovereign, he would have had a religious community, and that community would have been a religious church, *i. e.* a church professing godliness; and then, an obedient subject of civil government would not have been a complete member; and then, their institution would have been a religious institution; and then—what then? And then Mr. Booth's system would have gone to ruin. But he wisely foreseeing this, takes measures to secularize the whole. He begins at the head, and goes down to the institution. Jehovah must be a political sovereign, that the church may be political; the church must be political, that the membership may be so too; the membership must be political, that the institution may be political also. So all was political; a political sovereign, a political church, a political member, and a political institution. And now Mr. Booth has gained his point; for sure enough, there can be no analogy between a church and no church; and consequently no argument can be drawn in favour of infant membership from a church which never was, to a church that now exists. Yes, he has gained his point, he has run down infant baptism; but, at the same time, he has eradicated the church of God. Nay, he was under a necessity of eradicating the church of God, that infant baptism might be run down. This has given me a notion of infant baptism far different from what I ever had. And, if I could say, that any one thing has satisfied my mind respecting it more than another, it has been this: I saw that infant baptism could by no means be overthrown, without overthrowing the church of God. And for this conviction I am indebted to that very book, on which I have taken the liberty to animadvert. Nothing, therefore, in nature can be plainer than this consequence, that the system of Mr. Booth has subverted the church of God.

These are the three consequences which rise out of the Baptist system, and which, I have said, will operate to ruin that system out of which they arise: namely,

1. That, according to the principles and reasonings of the Baptists, a woman, however qualified, can have no right to the Lord's table.

2. That the Baptists, in opposing infant baptism, and defending female communion, do vary their mode of reasoning, contradict themselves, and prevaricate most wretchedly.

3. That, according to their principles and reasoning, God had no church in this world for many centuries.

I shall now close the Appendix by an appeal to the reader; and this I mean to do in three questions.

1. Are these consequences real? To answer this question I need only appeal to the Appendix itself. There the reader may satisfy himself respecting their reality. As to the first, it is there evident, that there is no explicit command for female communion; and, according to the Baptist system, they are not to commune without: the consequence is, that they have no right to commune at all. With regard to the second, I have placed Mr. Booth's defence of female communion against his opposition to infant baptism; and what repugnancy, prevarication, and self-contradiction, are discoverable in these two, I have presented to the reader. The third speaks openly for itself, that the best church in the world for many centuries, was nothing else but a civil government.

2. Do these consequences rise out of the Baptist system? For an answer to this I might refer the reader to the former part of the Appendix; where he may see in what way they actually do arise out of their system. Their system destroys the right of females to the Lord's supper, by demanding explicit proof for infant baptism; because there is no such proof for female communion. Their attempt to prove the right of females to commune, involves them in the most mean prevarication and self-contradiction. And in overthrowing the argument for infant bap-

tism taken from the membership of infants in God's ancient church, they overthrow the very church itself. In this way, these horrid consequences owe their birth to that bad system.

3. Are such consequences as these which rise out of the Baptist system, sufficient to ruin that system out of which they rise? To this I answer, that if any consequences are sufficient to ruin a system, these are they. It is a rule in reasoning, that that argument which proves too much destroys itself. The same is also true of a system; the system that proves too much must follow the fate of its kindred argument, and prove its own destruction. This system, it is true, proves against infant baptism; but there it does not stop, it carries its force still further; it proves against female communion, and against the existence of God's church; and to complete the whole, it proves against the author who patronizes it. So that if infant baptism fall, they all fall together; female communion falls, the church of God falls, the author himself, Mr. Booth, falls, and all by the same fatal system. For if this system makes infant baptism a nullity, it makes female communion a nullity too; and turns the church itself into a civil government, and turns the patron of it into a self-contradictor. This, if any thing can be, is proving too much; and, therefore, that system which is productive of such consequences, must itself be destroyed by the consequences it produces. And I appeal to the conscience of any reader

whether these consequences have not been proved, and whether they are not sufficient to destroy any system.

I call this a short method with the Baptists, because, whatever course they may take, it will serve to ruin their scheme. If, on the one hand, these consequences are suffered to remain as they do now in Mr. Booth's book, their scheme will be ruined this way. For that system can have no pretension at all to truth, which in its consequences militates against female communion, and the very existence of the church of God; and moreover exhibits the patron of it under the shape of a shifter, prevaricator, and self-contradictor. But if, on the other hand, they alter their mode of defence so as to avoid these consequences, their scheme will be ruined that way; for then, they will lose those very arguments by which they endeavour to support it. So that let a Baptist, Mr. Booth for instance, take which way he will, his scheme will either be overwhelmed with its own consequences, or it will fall for want of arguments.

Thus much I say at present concerning the Appendix; and shall now commit it into the hands of God, the eternal patron of truth, and to every reader's judgment and conscience in his sight.

A CASE

SUBMITTED TO THE CONSIDERATION OF BAPTISTS.

Before I enter on the Mode of Baptism, I would take the liberty of proposing to my Baptist friends a plain case; not so much a case of conscience as a case of criticism. That on which this case is founded is as follows: it is well known that under the present dispensation there are two instituted ordinances; the one in Scripture is expressed by the term *deipnon*, a supper, the other by *baptisma*, baptism. The proper and obvious meaning of *deipnon* is a feast or a common meal, Mark vi. 21; John xxi. 22; the proper meaning of *baptisma* is said to be the immersion of the whole body. The case then is this:

If, because the proper meaning of the term *baptisma*, baptism, is the immersion of the whole body, a person, who is not immersed, cannot be said to have been baptized, since nothing short of immersion amounts to the full import of the word baptism;—if this be true, I should be glad to know whether as *deipnon*, a supper, properly means a feast or common meal, a person who, in the use of that ordinance, takes only a piece of bread of half an inch square, and drinks a tablespoonfull of wine, which is neither a feast nor a common meal, and so does not come up to the proper meaning of the word, can be said to have received the Lord's Supper?

Mr. Booth, I presume, saw this in Mr. Piries' book, but has not taken any notice of it; I therefore request some Baptist friend to turn his attention to it.

THE MODE OF BAPTISM.

It appears to me, from the following circumstance, that the Baptists are not so tenacious of the mode as of the subject of baptism. I had been convinced more than four years ago, in reading Dr. Williams' book, that immersion was not essential to baptism; and though I preached since that period several baptizing sermons without saying a word about the mode, I never heard of any of our Baptist friends that ever observed that omission; whereas, on the contrary, had I insisted on the mode, and omitted the subject, I have not a doubt but they would have noticed it in the first sermon. And I remember some years back to have heard a Baptist minister say, that the mode of baptism, by immersion only, did not appear equally plain as the subject. Indeed I am persuaded that if it can be made plain to the Baptists that it is wrong to reject an infant, they will soon give up the idea of immersion only; and it is for this reason that I have been the more diffuse on the subject, and shall now be short on the mode.

All our knowledge of the manner of baptizing must, at this distance of time from the first institution, be collected from the word " baptize," the circumstances of baptism, and the allusions of Scripture to that ordinance. These three I will endeavour to examine impartially, confining myself to Scripture, and the word made use of in the institution. The question, on which this examination is to proceed, is this: is immersion essential to baptism? or, in other words, is there no baptism but what is by immersion? I shall begin the inquiry with that precise term which the Scriptures always use when this ordinance is spoke of, namely *baptizo*, and examine those places in which it occurs either as a noun or a verb, where the ordinance is not intended.

There is a word commonly introduced into this debate, *viz. bapto*, though it is never used in Scripture, respecting this ordinance; and this being the fact, I see no great propriety in bringing it into the debate at all; for let it mean what it may, it can signify nothing to the question in hand unless it had been used by the inspired writers to express this ordinance. I do not, however, shun this term because it would be unfavourable to my sentiment, but because I judge it best to examine that word, and that only, which the Holy Ghost, when speaking of this ordinance, has thought proper to adopt.

Nevertheless, that I may not omit it altogether, I would say thus much of the term *bapto*, that it is a term of such latitude, that he who shall attempt to prove, from its use in various authors, an absolute and total immersion, will find he has undertaken that which he can never fairly perform. Of the truth of this assertion I would give the plain reader a taste in the following instances. The term *bapto* then is used to express,

1. The throwing of a person into the mire. Job ix. 31. "Thou shalt plunge, (baptize) or make me foul in the mire."

2. A partial dipping. Matt. xxvi. 23. "He that dippeth (baptizeth) his hand with me in the dish."

3. A stained garment. Rev. xix. 13. "A vesture dipped (baptized) stained with blood."

4. A human body wet with the dew. Dan. iv. 33. "His body was wet (baptized) by or from the dew of heaven."

5. The colouring a lake with the blood of a frog. Homer, "The lake was baptized, coloured, or stained with blood."

6. The smearing of the face with colours or washes. Aristophanes, "He baptized, smeared [his face] with tawney washes;" speaking of Magnes, the comedian, who used to colour his face instead of using a mask.

7. The staining of the hand by pressing a substance; Aristotle, "Being pressed, it baptizes, stains the hand."

So various is the use of the term *bapto*, that we can only view it as meaning to w t or stain, and that by whatever mode the nature of the thing to be wetted or stained may require. And I can truly say I have often been heartily sick and sorry when I have observed persons of eminence for learning, especially Dr. Gale, labouring, in opposition to the very instances which they themselves had produced, to prove that this term intended immersion, total immersion, and nothing else. But as this word is never used with respect to the ordinance in question, and can therefore give us no information concerning the mode of it, I shall immediately dismiss it without further notice.

I come now to consider the term *baptizo*, which is the only term made use of to express this ordinance, and this I shall do by setting down those places where it is used as a verb or a noun when the ordinance is not intended. These places are as follow: Heb ix. 10. "Which stood in meats and drinks and divers washings — divers baptisms." Mark vii. 4. "And when they come from the market, except they wash (except they baptize) they eat not. And many other things there be which they have received to hold, as the washing, (baptisms) of cups and pots, brazen vessels and of tables." Luke xi. 38. "And when the Pharisee saw it, he marvelled that he had not first washed, (baptized) before dinner." The word in these instances, is used,

1. For those various ablutions among the Jews, by sprinkling, pouring, &c.

2. For a custom among the Pharisees of washing before meals.

3. For a superstitious washing of household furniture, cups, pots, &c.

With these instances in view, I would propose to the reader two questions:

I. Is the word baptize used in these instances to express immersion only? The reader may observe that the very first instance proves it is not. The Apostle plainly expresses the Jewish ablutions by the term " baptisms;" and any man, by looking into his Bible, and reading the account of the Jewish service, may see what kind of baptisms these were. Mr. Booth himself, in his answer to Dr. Williams, p. 347, will grant for the sake of argument, that the apostle uses the term baptisms in this place to denote pouring and sprinkling as well as immersion; nor does he, in what he has advanced on the subject, deny this to have been the fact; and indeed a man must be very defective in point of modesty who will even attempt to deny this. Well then, if the word baptism is not used in these instances, as it is certain it is not, to express immersion only, I ask, in the next place—Is it used to express any immersion at all? I will apply this question to each of the instances:

1. The Apostle speaks of the Jewish service, and says it stood in " divers baptisms." I ask whether immersion of the whole body was any part of that service? It is clear that the Apostle, by the word " baptisms," intended sprinkling and pouring; but I believe it is not clear from any part of the

Jewish service, that any one was ordered to immerse himself, or to be immersed by another. If this, however, can be proved, it must then be granted that the Apostle uses the word "baptisms" to denote immersion as well as pouring and sprinkling; but if this cannot be proved, it will then be evident that no immersion at all is intended by the word baptisms.

2. I will apply the question to the second case—the baptizing before meals. It is said, "that when they come from market, except they baptize they eat not;" and the "Pharisee marvelled that our Lord did not baptize (that is, himself) before dinner." I ask, Is there any immersion at all here? The Pharisee marvelled that our Lord did not baptize himself before dinner—did he marvel that he did not immerse himself? The Pharisees, when they come from market, except they baptize [themselves] they eat not—did they too immerse themselves every time they came from a market? I know it is not an impossible case; but I am asking whether it is at all a probable thing? And if it be not, then it is improbable that the word baptize in these places should intend any immersion at all. Perhaps some one will say that nothing more is intended than the washing of hands, as this is agreeable to the tradition of the elders mentioned in Matt. xv. 2.; and it is well known that we dip our hands in order to wash them. Supposing this to be the fact, I reply, that if we dip our hands in order to

baptize [wash] them, then it is certain, that dipping and baptizing [washing] are different things;—that baptizing [washing] is the end, and dipping a mean to that end;—that we only dip so much of our hands as may be necessary to baptize [wash] them;—and that our dipping the hands in order to baptize them depends entirely on circumstances: *e. g.* If I baptize [wash] my hands in a basin, I dip so much of them as may be necessary to baptize them; but if I baptize [wash] them at a spout, I do not dip them at all—I only receive the water as it falls, and baptize [wash] them without dipping. And it signifies nothing to us how they baptized [washed] their hands, whether in a basin or at a spout; for the word " baptize" does not express the manner of doing, whether by immersion or affusion, but only the thing done, namely, " washing."

3. I now carry the question to the third case—the superstitious baptizing [washing] of household furniture, cups, pots, brazen vessels, and tables. Cups; these, it appears from the name, were drinking vessels; pots; those vessels out of which wine or water was poured, pitchers or flagons. Brazen vessels, were, it is probable, for culinary uses, for boiling. Tables, some take this word as it is here rendered, others think it means those seats or benches on which they sat at meals; and these are sometimes called " *lecti*" beds, perhaps from the leaning posture then in use. The Jews, our Lord ob-

serves, held and practised the baptizing of these; now we ask, Does the word baptize in this place express any immersion?

These things, it is plain, were baptized [washed;] but how they were baptized, no creature living can determine. One thing, however, may be remarked, which is, that all these articles might very conveniently be baptized [washed] by pouring, &c. while, on the contrary, it would have been very inconvenient, and even improper, to baptize [wash] others, *viz.* the brazen vessels and tables, by immersion. It is, I believe, a general opinion that some of these things were baptized by dipping—as the cups and pots, and that others were baptized [washed] by pouring, sprinkling, &c. And hence many learned men have considered the word baptize as expressing all these modes. In this, however, they appear to me to have been mistaken; for the word baptize, [wash] though it has been applied to all modes of washing, is not properly expressive of any mode, but intends only the washing itself, which may be done by either.

The conclusion, therefore, from these instances, is this: it is evident that the word baptize does not intend immersion only; the various sprinklings, pourings, &c. among the Jews are plainly called "baptism." Nay, further, it is not certain that there was any immersion at all in either of the baptisms [washings] before us; and it is very certain that whether these persons and things were baptized by immersion, aspersion, or affusion, the word baptize does not express either of the modes by which any person or thing was washed, but only the washing itself. And though there has been much dispute about the word "baptize," some affirming it to mean immersion only, others aspersion and affusion as well as immersion, yet, properly speaking, it means neither of them. It has indeed been used for all the modes of washing—sprinkling, pouring, and immersing; whereas it does not express the one nor the other, but washing only; and this may be done in either of the modes; and, therefore, when we read of any person or thing being baptized, we cannot conclude from the word itself whether it was done by affusion, aspersion, or immersion.

As the word "baptize," which means simply to wash, does not determine the mode in which persons should receive baptism, I will attend in the next place, to the circumstances of that ordinance. Those I mean to consider are, first, the places where baptism was administered, and, secondly, the preparations for baptism.

1. The places chosen for this ordinance were, among others, the river Jordan, and Enon near Salim, where, it is said, there were many waters. This is a circumstance that appears to weigh on the side of immersion; and if we give it that weight in the scale of reason, for which the Baptists contend, it will amount to this—it is a presump-

tive, but not a certain, proof of immersion. That it is a presumptive proof appears by this—that here was, as far as we know, a fair opportunity for immersion; that it is no more than a presumptive proof is evident from hence—that all this might be, and yet no immersion. If we say they baptized in or at a river, therefore they baptized by immersion, this would be a good consequence if it were impossible to baptize at or in a river in any other way; but since a person can baptize in or at a river by affusion as well as immersion, we can only draw a conclusion in favour of immersion by an act of the fancy. However, let it be a proof of the presumptive kind, and it cannot possibly be any thing more.

Now, as it is the nature of presumptive proof to admit of increase or diminution, this, like all proof of the same kind, may be increased or diminished. That, on the one hand, which serves to increase the presumption on the side of immersion, is this: that of all who administer baptism, there are none at this time (as far as I know) that baptize in or at a river, but such as use immersion. It may indeed be said that all this may be accounted for. The case of John differed very much from ours; he had vast congregations and many to baptize, and no house fit to contain them: so that his choosing a river, though he had baptized by affusion, would, in his case, have been, on the whole, the wisest plan. And although persons who baptize by affusion, do not now go to a river, yet were they circumstanced, with respect to their congregations and accommodations, as John was, they would, in their choice of place, act in the same manner he did. Something like this, I suppose, might be said, but I was willing to give the presumption all its force.

On the other hand, the presumption may be diminished by observing, first, that there were many baptizings which do not appear to have taken place at or in any river—as that of Paul, of the jailer, of Cornelius, of those of Samaria, and of the three thousand. And, secondly, there is another thing: it cannot be proved with certainty that even those who were baptized in or at Jordan, Enon, &c. were—I will not say totally immersed, but that they were so much as in the water at all. Whoever is acquainted with the indeterminate sense of the prepositions *en, eis*,* *ek*, and *apo*, on which this proof must depend, will be very sensible of this. These occur in the following Scriptures: Matt. iii. 6. " They were baptized of him, *en to Iordanee*, in Jordan ;"—*en* means not only " in," but " nigh, near, at, by," &c. Acts viii. 38. " They went down both, *eis to hudor*, into the water ;" but *eis*, besides " into," often means

---

* John xx. 4, 5, came first *to* [*eis*] the sepulchre—Yet went he not in. From which it is evident that *eis* signifies *to* as well as *into ;* and therefore to pretend to determine the mode of baptism from the signification of that word is trifling.

"towards, near," &c. Matt. iii. 16. "And Jesus when he was baptized, went up straightway, *apo tou hudatos*, out of the water." Acts viii. 39. "And when they were come up, *ek tou hudatos*, out of the water;"—*apo* and *ek* very often signify "from." So that whereas it is read in our translation — in Jordan, into the water, out of the water, it will read as well in the Greek—at Jordan, to the water, from the water. This is a truth beyond all dispute, and well known to every one who is at all conversant with the Greek. And whoever duly considers this will easily be persuaded that it is utterly impossible to prove that any one, who is said in Scripture to have been baptized, was so much as in the water at all, or that he even wet the sole of his foot.

2. The other circumstance relates to a preparation for the ordinance. Every one who has been accustomed to baptize by immersion, must certainly know, that it is necessary, with respect to decency and safety, to change the dresses, and to have separate apartments for men and women. This is evidently necessary, whether we baptize in a river, or in a baptistry. Now it is certain, that although we read of many baptizings, there is not the least intimation given either of changing the dress, or of any suitable accommodation for the different sexes. This, though a circumstance that weighs against immersion, I consider as being, like the other, only of the presumptive kind. For, no doubt

it would be very illogical to say, we read of no change of dress, or separate apartments for baptizing, therefore there was no immersion.

This presumption, like the other, may be made stronger or weaker. It may be made weaker in this way; that though we read of no changing of garments, or any separate apartments, yet there might have been both; as many things might have been done of which the Scriptures take no notice. On the other side, the presumption may be made stronger, by observing that there are other cases in which mention is made of garments, where there could be no more necessity of mentioning them, than in the case of baptism; supposing baptism to have been performed by immersion. To instance only in two cases; when our Lord washed his disciples' feet, it is said, he laid aside his garments. And Luke, speaking of those who stoned Stephen, says, " they laid down their clothes at a young man's feet, whose name was Saul." Now if the Scriptures take notice of the putting off of garments for the purpose of washing feet, and stoning a man to death; how comes it to pass, that as thousands, upon supposition they were baptized by immersion, must entirely have changed their garments, or have done worse, the Scriptures should not drop a single hint about it? Both these presumptions may be tossed and turned, and strengthened and weakened, just as fancy may dictate; whereas, when all is said and done, they are no more than presumptions still. And when we have only presumption in the premises, we can have nothing more than presumption in the conclusion.

To conclude this part respecting the circumstances of baptism, I will only say, we have here a goodly combat; presumption contending with presumption. One presumption says, that as they sometimes made use of a river for baptizing, it is likely they baptized by immersion. The other presumption answers, that since it does not appear, that the sexes were decently accommodated for immersion, or that there was any changing of garments, it is therefore likely they did not immerse. That presumption replies, that the sexes might be very decently accommodated with change of dress, and separate apartments, though the Scriptures should notice neither. This presumption affirms, that persons might be baptized in or at a river, and yet no immersion after all.

Now instead of determining which of these presumptions is the stronger; we may learn thus much from the circumstances of baptism, and indeed it is all we can learn, and that is, that it is utterly impossible to determine, from any information they give, whether baptized persons were immersed or not. Nay, so far are circumstances from settling this point, that we cannot be certain there was a single person of all the baptized, who went into the water even ankle deep. This is the true state of facts as they strike me, and all beyond this is the flight of fancy.

Since neither the term "baptize," nor yet the circumstances of baptism, determine any thing concerning the mode, whether it is immersion or affusion; I shall in the next place consider the allusions to that ordinance. I know not whether I speak accurately when I call them allusions; but the consequence either way is not material, as every one will easily understand what I intend. Now these allusions being of two kinds, I will, for the sake of distinction, and without any design of offence, call one the "Baptist allusion," and the other the "Pædobaptist allusion." I begin with,

I. The Baptist allusion. The reader will find this in Rom. vi. 4. "Therefore we are buried with him by baptism into death," &c. A similar phrase occurs in Col. ii. 12. The Baptists think there is an allusion in these words to the manner of baptizing; and as the apostle speaks of being buried with him, they conclude the mode to have been immersion. On this conclusion of theirs,

1. I observe that these words are an inference from the third verse, in which the apostle says, "Know ye not that so many of us as were baptized into Jesus Christ were baptized into his death? Therefore we are buried with him by baptism." We have here three things; 1. a baptizing into Jesus Christ; 2. into his death; 3. into his burial

and the last is made the consequence of the first. Therefore we are buried with him, because we were baptized into him. To form the antithesis, we must distinguish between the life and death of Christ; and then it will be, We are baptized first into the life of Christ, then into the death of Christ, and last of all into his burial. We are brought by baptism into his life, into his death, and into his burial. Now, if baptism bring us into each of these, and one of them, as the Baptists say, is an allusion to the mode of baptizing, then, for the same reason, so must the other two. That is, his life must allude to the mode, so must his death, and so must his burial; and the reason is, because baptism unites us to him in each of these. And if all these are to allude to the mode, I should be glad to know, what kind of mode it must at last be, which is to bear a resemblance to every one. The life of Christ was action, his death was a crucifixion, his burial was the inclosing of his body in a cavity of the rock. The mode, therefore, must be threefold; it must represent action, crucifixion, and inclosing in a rock; because, to pursue the notion of the Baptists, his life, death, and burial must all have an allusion to the mode of baptism.

There is no sect, I should suppose, that uses a mode of baptism to which all these will agree. The Romanists use salt, oil, and spittle; but whether they intend an allusion to the life of Christ, I cannot take upon me to affirm. Yet, as they must have some allusion, the salt may allude to his life of teaching; the spittle to his life of miracles; and the oil to his life of munificence. The clergy of the church of England use the sign of the cross; and this is to allude to the crucifixion of Christ. The Baptists use immersion: and this is to allude to the burial of Christ. Now, if we could unite all these in one, we should have a tolerable allusion to our Lord's life, death, and burial; but when each is taken separately, there is a deficiency in point of allusion. The English clergy are deficient in alluding only to the crucifixion; but not to the life and burial. The Romanists are deficient in alluding only to the life and crucifixion; but not to the burial. The Baptists too are deficient in alluding to the burial only; but not to the life and crucifixion. I know not whether these different communities take their document from this part of holy writ; but certainly they have the same ground if they choose to reason in the same way. But as the Baptists avowedly do this, and are at the same time so deficient in the business of allusion, it would become them to set about a reform in the mode of their baptism; it being at present wanting in two articles, viz. the life and crucifixion, i. e. the sign of the cross, and salt, &c.

That the absurdity of supposing an allusion in this place to the mode of baptism may appear in a still stronger light, I would observe, that what the apostle calls, in ver. 3

a being baptized into the death of Christ, he expresses in ver. 5, by being planted together in the likeness of his death. This will be evident to any one who examines the place. Now if any man is disposed, after the method of the Baptists, to pick up allusions to the mode of baptism, here are two topics ready at hand, and he may take both, or either, as he pleases. It is usual with the Baptists, when contending for the mode of baptism, to affirm that the apostle calls baptism a burial; and hence they infer that immersion must be the mode. This, however, is affirming what is not true; for the apostle never, in any of his writings, calls "baptism a burial." But on the contrary, he does in this verse evidently speak of it under the notion of planting; and says, We are planted in the likeness of his death. Here then, upon the Baptist plan, are two allusions—planting, and crucifixion. There are none, I believe, who make planting an allusion to the mode of baptism; but should this be attempted by any, they will have this one advantage which the Baptists are destitute of; and that is, that whereas baptism is no where called a burial, it is in this place plainly called a planting. Now, if we suppose a person reasoning upon the plan of the Baptists, he will say, that as the apostle calls baptism a planting, he must allude to the mode in which that ordinance was administered; and every one, who is at all acquainted with the art of planting, will easily guess what kind of mode that must be, to which it alludes. Were this only adopted, and it may be adopted with greater advantage than the Baptist plan, we should probably hear of some contention about the mode of baptism, between those who immerse and those who only plant; and in this case I can clearly see that victory will crown the planters.

There is in the same way another allusion in this verse to the mode of baptism; I have mentioned it before, but do it again on account of its superior evidence to that allusion of the Baptists. The apostle says, we are planted, that is, baptized, in the likeness of his death. Now, taking this for an allusion to the mode of baptism, the argument for the sign of the cross will be incomparably stronger than that of the Baptists for immersion. I say incomparably stronger; for whereas it is only said in the fourth verse, We are buried with him *by* baptism; it is said in this verse, We are planted [baptized] in the likeness of his death: there is nothing about similitude mentioned in their allusion; but here the word "likeness" is actually used. The argument, therefore, in favour of the sign of the cross, will, in the Baptist way of arguing, far outweigh that in favour of immersion. And how much soever the Baptists may despise that ceremony, it is evidently better founded in this contest than their own. So that if their argument from this place be good for immersion, the other is far better for the sign of the cross. Upon the whole, the examination of this place convinces me of nothing so much as this, that both the Baptists in general, and myself in particular, have been carried away with the mere sound of a word, even to the neglect of the sense and scope of the truth of God.

2. Leaving, therefore, the whimsical interpretation of the Baptists to itself, it may be observed, in order that we may the better enter into the apostle's design, that when he says, "we are buried with him, by baptism," he makes baptism to be the instrumental cause of burial. This will appear plain by asking this question; By what are we buried with him? The answer is, By baptism. And indeed baptism is made the instrumental cause in each case. If we ask, How are we brought into Jesus Christ? Answer—By baptism: "baptized into Jesus Christ." How are we brought into his death? Answer—By baptism: "baptized into his death." How are we brought into his burial? Answer—By baptism: "buried with him by baptism." If, therefore, the union in life, death, and burial, be brought about by baptism, then baptism is the instrumental cause of this union; and then the very idea of allusion is entirely lost, and they present themselves to our view under the notion of cause and effect. Baptism is made the cause, and union in the life, death, and burial, the effect.

Now this being the case, instead of hunting after allusions, by which baptism will be any thing or nothing, we must attend to that adequacy or proportion in the cause, by virtue of which this effect is to be produced. This adequacy is not formally in outward baptism, which is an emblem, and no more than an emblem, of the baptism of the Holy Spirit; but merely in the baptism of the Holy Spirit, of which the other is an emblem. 1 Cor. xii. 13. It is, indeed, the nature and design of both to bring persons into union with Jesus Christ; but then, the union will be only of the same kind with the baptism. If the baptism be that of the Holy Spirit, it brings about an internal, vital union with Jesus Christ; but if it be only an outward baptism, the union will only be visible and external. But as the outward baptism is an emblem of the inward and vital, the judgment of charity presumes, unless there be good proof to the contrary, that they who voluntarily receive the former, are also possessed of the latter. It is according to this judgment of charity, the apostle addresses the Romans: he supposes baptized persons to be really baptized into Jesus Christ; and then, by virtue of that union, they live, they die, they are buried, they are raised again, and walk with Christ in newness of life. All which the apostle expresses in these emphatic words:—our old man is crucified with him, that the body of sin might be destroyed, that henceforth we should not serve sin— Dead indeed unto sin, but alive unto God through Jesus Christ our Lord — Like as Christ was raised from the dead, by the glory of the Father, even so we also should walk in newness of life. The scope of the apostle is to show the vital influence of union with Christ, of which baptism is the emblem. And as soon as any one enters fairly into the apostle's scope, the insignificant idea of allusion to the mode of baptism disappears, and, to use Mr. Booth's phrase, hides its impertinent head.—Thus much for the Baptist allusion. I shall next notice,

II. The Pædobaptist allusion. According to this, the mode of communicating the grace of the Holy Spirit to the soul, and that of applying the baptismal water to the body, are viewed as corresponding with each other. The considerations which lead to this, are such as follow:—1. They both agree in name. The influences of the Holy Spirit on the soul are called " baptism," and so likewise is the external application of water. The term baptism, when used to express the influences of the Holy Spirit, takes in both his extraordinary and saving influences, Acts i. 5; 1 Cor. xii. 13. And as these have sometimes taken place in the same persons, the term " baptize" has been used to express both, Acts x. 44—46, compared with Acts xi. 16—18. 2. They are often associated in Scripture. How commonly do we read such words as these, " I indeed have baptized you with water; but he shall baptize you with the Holy Ghost." The reader will find this form of speech in the following places: Matt. iii. 11. Mark i. 8. Luke iii. 16. John i. 33.

Acts i. 5; xi. 16. 3. Their mode of communication is expressed in the same way: "I baptize you with water, but he shall baptize you with the Holy Ghost." And this is done in all the places, only with this difference, that Luke omits the preposition in one member, and there it is understood. 4. Baptism with water, is an emblem of baptism with the Holy Ghost. The application of water to the body, as noting the putting away the filth of the flesh, shadows forth the influence of the Holy Spirit, which, being imparted to the soul, produces the answer of a good conscience towards God.

Now, if these two pass under the same name; if both are frequently united in Scripture; if the one be an emblem of the other; and if the mode of communication in each baptism be expressed in the same way; then, the way to arrive at a clear view of the mode of outward baptism, is to observe in what manner the baptism of the Holy Spirit is described. This will lead us to consult a lexicon of very superior kind, a lexicon worth more than five hundred; and, what is more, it is the plain, unlettered man's lexicon, and its title is, "The lively oracles of God." The article we are to seek for, is the term baptize. How does this lexicon define *baptizare*, to baptize? Answer—*Baptizare est supervenire, illabi, effundere*—plainly, to baptize is —to come upon, Acts i. 5.—to shed forth, Acts ii. 33.—to fall upon, Acts xi. 15.—to pour out, Acts ii. 17.—x. 45. That is, in this baptism, the grace of the Holy Spirit comes upon—falls upon—is shed forth—is poured out, namely, on the soul. This is the account this lexicon gives of the word " baptize."

Mr. Booth instead of paying a due attention to this lexicon, has adopted a method which, when properly adverted to, will do no credit to him or his book. His professed design is to prove that the term " baptize" means immersion, immersion only, and nothing else. But how does he do it? Why, he quotes a number of authors, who, as he himself says, understood the term to mean immersion, pouring, and sprinkling; and these quotations he calls concessions. Concessions of what? That the word meant immersion only? If so, he made them concede what they never did concede, and what they had no thought of conceding. If they made no concession, as he acknowledges they did not, that the term baptize signified immersion only, what honesty could there be in producing them at all? Mr. Booth's talent is quotation, and therefore he must quote; but, at the same time, it is a shame to abuse the living or the dead, and it is a bad cause that requires it; for what else is it but abusing an author, when he is introduced as granting that which in fact he never did grant?

But had Mr. Booth consulted the lexicon I am speaking of, it might have freed him from the necessity of using that little art which one cannot observe in a disputant with any degree of pleasure The authors he has consulted, if they had been all on his side, (and I question whether any one was beside the Quakers) could only have told him how men understood the word; but this lexicon would have showed him how God himself uses it; and if we receive the witness of men, the witness of God is greater. I ask, What does God witness concerning the term baptize? Answer—From the passages before cited it is evident he witnesses this—that the term strictly and properly means to wash, to purify. What does God witness concerning the mode of applying the purifying matter? Answer—It comes upon, falls upon, is shed forth, is poured out.—Why then, as water baptism is an emblem of this, and as the mode of application in both cases is expressed in the same way, we have a witness on the side of pouring and sprinkling in baptism infinitely more certain than that of all the lexicographers and critics in the world. What are Mr. Booth's eighty abused critics, even supposing they had all been on his side, though I doubt whether he had one out of the eighty; and even suppose he had eight hundred more, what, I say, are all these when compared to the all-wise God expounding and defining of his own words? Mr. Booth has a Talmud of his own, in which he studies circumcision, and ill-treated critics, with whom he imposes on the public in the article of baptism; and though perhaps he may not yet be ashamed of his Talmud, or his treatment, I believe the time will come when he will be ashamed of both.

Notwithstanding the Scriptures, when speaking of the baptism of the Holy Spirit, make use of the phrases—come upon—fall upon—shed forth—poured out, Mr. Booth, to evade the force of this as it respects the mode of baptizing, has recourse to two miserable shifts. In one case he would set aside the allusion to the mode, and in the other he would make it agree with immersion; and as these are somewhat curious, I cannot very well close the subject without taking notice of them.

1. To set aside the allusion, he takes the following course in his answer to Dr. Williams. Page 341, he says, "Dr. Williams argues in favour of pouring and of sprinkling from the baptism of the Holy Spirit. Thus he speaks: I scruple not to assert it, there is no object whatever in all the New Testament so frequently and so explicitly signified by baptism as these divine influences;" referring to Matt. iii. 11.; Mark i. 8, 9.; Luke iii. 16. 21, 22; and several other places. Mr. Booth, in answer, says, p. 342, "But those passages of Scripture to which he refers, regard that copious and extraordinary effusion (effusion, *i. e.* pouring out) of the Holy Spirit which was received by the Apostles and first disciples of our Lord soon after his ascension into heaven." The truth is, the term "baptize," when applied to the Holy Spirit, is used to denote both his extraordinary and ordinary influ-

ences, even those by which the mind is renewed and united to Christ; and so baptism by affusion is the most expressive emblem of the communication of these influences, more especially as the mode of application is expressed in the same way, and the one is fairly an emblem of the other.

But Mr. Booth does not seem willing to admit that one baptism is an emblem of the other—I say, "seem willing," for I protest I do not know, though I have his book before my eyes, and have looked at it half an hour, whether he means to admit or deny it. That which seems the most evident is, he wishes, by any means, to get rid of it, lose it, put it out of sight, forget it himself, and make his reader do so too; but then how is this to be done? Done! why, by the assistance of his old impartial friends the Quakers. He suggests that our viewing water baptism as an emblem of the baptism of the Holy Spirit, will operate against its perpetuity. To evince this he introduces the Quakers as reasoning in the following manner: "water baptism was divinely appointed, and continued in force till the death of Christ; but as that rite had for its object the descent of the Holy Spirit and his divine influences, no sooner was the promised Spirit vouchsafed to our Lord's disciples, than the obligation to regard water baptism entirely ceased. For baptism in water being only an emblem of the promised baptism in the Holy Spirit, why should the former be continued after the latter has taken place?" This, he says, or something like it, if he mistakes not, is the Quakers' principal argument; and, for aught he perceives, it is equally forcible with that of his opponent.

I confess I am not sufficiently versed in the Quakers' mode of reasoning to know whether Mr. Booth has done them justice. He first makes them say that baptism continued till the death of Christ, and then that the obligation to regard it ceased when the promised Spirit was vouchsafed. So there are two periods for the expiration of baptism. But I have no dispute with the Quakers; I know they are only brought in here as a blind, that Mr. Booth, by getting behind them, might withdraw more easily. I am persuaded he does not approve of their argument—he only wanted to get rid of the allusion, and he has got rid of it; but it is in the same way as the Quakers get rid of the two ordinances. Nay, far worse; for they do this by arguments which they deem good, but Mr. Booth has done it by such reasoning as he himself would be ashamed to adopt. This is Mr. Booth's miserable way of getting rid of the allusion, *viz.* by giving the reader a Quaker's argument. I will now advert to his other shift, by which,

2. He attempts to make the allusion agree with immersion. The mode, as I have before said, of communicating the influence of the Holy Spirit, is in Scripture expressed by coming upon —falling upon—shedding forth

—pouring out, and this mode of communication is expressly called baptizing. Now, while most persons have considered the baptism of the Holy Spirit as favouring affusion, Mr. Booth will undertake to show that it is expressive of that idea for which he contends, namely, immersion. This is an attempt in which I could wish him much success; for if he can make it appear that pouring out, and immersing into, are the same thing, then neither will he have any reason to complain of those that pour, nor will those who pour have any reason to complain of him. I fear it will prove a hard task; let us hear him, however.

In vol. i. p. 101, he speaks of "an electrical bath, so called, because the electrical fluid surrounds the patient." Well, and what then? "This philosophical document reminds me of the sacred historian's language, where, narrating the fact under consideration, thus he speaks: 'And when the day of Pentecost was fully come, they were all with one accord in one place. And suddenly there came a sound from heaven as of a rushing mighty wind, and it FILLED ALL THE HOUSE WHERE THEY WERE SITTING. And there appeared unto them cloven tongues like as of fire, and it sat upon each of them. And they were all filled with the Holy Ghost.' Now, says he, if the language of medical electricity be just, it cannot be absurd, nay, it seems highly rational, to understand this language of inspiration, as expressive of that idea [immersion] for which we contend. Was the Holy Spirit poured out? Did the Holy Spirit fall upon the apostles and others at that memorable time? It was in such a manner and to such a degree, that they were, like a patient in the electric bath, as if immersed in it."

This electric bath is a pretty fancy, a happy invention for Mr. Booth; it is well he did not live before it was found out, for then what a fine thought would have been lost! Though the Holy Spirit fell upon, was poured out, yet, says he, it was in such a manner and to such a degree, that they were, like a patient in the electric bath, as if immersed in it, that is, immersed in the Holy Spirit. Most persons, I suppose, when they read of the Holy Spirit falling upon any one, understand it to mean the influence of that Spirit coming upon the soul; but Mr. Booth speaks as if the Holy Ghost, or his influence, fell on the outside of the apostles, and so surrounded their bodies like an electric bath. And to show he intended this, he has put these words in large capitals, it " FILLED ALL THE HOUSE WHERE THEY WERE SITTING." Then they were immersed in something which filled the house; I ask, what was that something? In English it is expressed by the pronoun "it"—it filled the house; the Greek has no pronoun. Well, what is the antecedent to "it?" I answer, the word "sound." The sound, which was as a rushing mighty wind, filled all the house where they were sitting. The word in the Greek is, *cechos*, an echo, a reverberating sound. Mr. Booth's electric bath was, after all, nothing more than an echo. He has been very silent about this electric fluid; either he did not know what it was, or he was not complaisant enough to tell us. The loss, however, is not great; we have found it out without him. It was an echo, then, that filled all the house; and the apostles, being immersed in sound, were surrounded by the echo, like a patient in an electric bath. This is the beauty of sticking close to the primary meaning of the term, as Mr. Booth calls it; and so tenacious is he of his primary meaning, that he does not care in what people are immersed, so they are but immersed in something.

To be baptized by the Holy Spirit is to receive his influence on the heart and mind; but this baptism, according to Mr. Booth, is to have the body surrounded by an echo. Is then the influence of the Spirit falling upon the heart, and a reverberating sound surrounding the body, the same thing? Mr. Booth is a dreadful confounder of things that differ! He said once that an obedient subject of the civil government and a complete church member were the same thing; does he think too that the influence of the Holy Ghost is nothing more than an echo?—So much for the electric bath and the Quaker's argument? These are Mr. Booth's two miserable shifts, by which he would evade the argument from the Holy Spirit's baptism in favour of affusion; and miserable ones they are as ever made their appearance in public.

I shall now close what I mean to say on the mode, by collecting the particulars, and placing them in one view. The word *baptizo*, used for this ordinance, means washing only, but not any mode of washing: it means neither dipping, pouring, nor sprinkling; for these are only different ways of washing, *i. e.* baptizing. They, therefore, who say that the word rantism [sprinkling] is not the same as baptism, say nothing but what is very right; for rantize differs from baptize, as the manner of doing differs from the thing done; and the same is true of immersion and pouring. Yet, at the same time, it must be observed that the word baptism is used in Scripture where pouring and sprinkling are evidently intended; while it cannot be proved that it is ever used either in the New Testament or in the Septuagint where immersion took place. The New Testament I have examined; I will here just notice the two places where it occurs in the Septuagint. 2 Kings, v. 14. And Naaman went down and baptized in Jordan. The English has it "dipped," and this is the only place where baptize is translated "dip;" but whether there was an immersion of the whole body, or any part of it, is altogether uncertain. All we can be certain of is, that the prophet ordered him to wash, his servants advised him to wash, and he went down and baptized according to the word of Elisha. Now there are two reasons which induce some to think he applied water to one part of his body only: 1. As he expected the prophet to strike his hand over the place, and recover the leper, they conclude he was leprous only in one part of his body, and that the water was applied to that part. 2. The command to wash seven times, they consider as referring to that part of the law of cleansing in which the leper is ordered to be sprinkled; but, for my own part, I think it impossible to say in what manner he baptized. The other is merely figurative, expressive of a sense of God's anger, and occurs in Isaiah xxi. 4. " And sin baptizes me;" meaning the punishment due to sin, which is expressed by pouring out anger, fury, &c. on a person. From these premises the unforced conclusion is this: that, on the one hand, as the word baptize is expressive of no particular mode, nothing can be concluded from it in favour of one more than another; so, on the other hand, as the word has certainly been used for pouring and sprinkling, while there is no proof of its ever being used in Scripture for immersion, it does more naturally associate itself with affusion and aspersion. With regard to the circumstances of baptism, they afford no certain proof on either side. We can do no more than presume, and this may be done on both sides. There is presumption for or against, and fancy, as it may happen to favour any one side, will form the conclusion; but as the circumstances carry us no further than presumption, no certain conclusion can be formed either for immersion or against it. The allusions, I observed, were of two kinds; the one I have called the Baptist allusion, the other the Pædobaptist allusion. The Baptist allusion is entirely founded in mistake, and that through a non-attention to the design and scope of the apostle; for in the same way as the Baptists make an allusion to immersion, the context will furnish allusions to other modes: and disputants, were they so inclined, might plead with more advantage for the sign of the cross, &c. than the Baptists can for immersion. The Pædobaptists' allusion consists in this: they consider the two baptisms, the material and the spiritual, as being the one a shadow or figure of the other, and the mode of the material as resembling that of the spiritual. And, therefore, as divine influence in spiritual baptism is said to come upon—fall upon—to be shed forth—poured out, and as material baptism is to be a significant emblem of this, the allusion is decidedly in favour of pouring and sprinkling. And that this is the true state of the matter appears by this: that the Scriptures commonly join material and spiritual baptism together as counterparts of each other, and express them by the same word, and describe them, as to their mode, in the same way. The consequence then is, that as the baptism of the Spirit is pouring, shedding, &c., and as the baptism of water is to represent that, and is described, as to its mode, in the same way, that mode must of necessity be pouring or sprinkling.

THE USE OF INFANT BAPTISM.

As I have often heard it asked, What is the use of infant baptism? I think it necessary, before I conclude, to say something in answer to that question. With regard to the use of baptism I consider it in the light of a mean of grace, and I view it in the same way when applied to infants. I do not suppose that infants, properly speaking, receive any present benefit by being baptized, but that this is designed the more to engage the attention of parents, and others to the rising generation. I view infants, when baptized, under the notion of persons entered into a school; and, therefore, I consider parents, pastors, and deacons, and church-members, at large, as brought under an additional obligation to instruct those children who are become scholars, as they become able to learn, in the peculiar truths of the religion of Christ. Viewing the matter in this light, it assumes an importance exceedingly grand; and infant baptism is far from being that unmeaning thing, which it appears to be, when the views are extended no further than helpless infancy.

We may illustrate this by taking a view of circumcision. Circumcision brought persons under an obligation of conforming to the revealed will of God; he who was circumcised became a debtor: and as this was the nature of the institution, the obligation devolved on all who received it. But for as much as persons cannot actually conform before they are brought to understand, and, in order that they may understand, they must be taught, we are, therefore, to consider circumcised infants as standing in the place of scholars or disciples to be instructed in that system to which they were bound to conform. If then circumcision brought an obligation on some to learn, it must, at the same time, bring an obligation on others to teach; because usually persons do not learn without being taught: and hence parents, priests, and people, came under their respective degrees of obligation to see the rising generation instructed in that religion into which they were initiated as scholars or disciples. When I consider this divine institution as calculated to fix the attention of the people on their rising offspring, with respect to their instruction in the things of God, I cannot sufficiently wonder at that poor heathenish notion of circumcision which Mr. Booth has somewhere picked up, or rather invented himself, than which, I am persuaded, the most ignorant Jew never entertained a meaner.

It is for want of viewing the matter in this way, that an institution, administered to an infant, appears ridiculous to any. When the attention is fixed on the infant only, whether it be a circumcised or a baptized infant, without considering any thing further, we may well say, as the Baptists do, What can an infant know? What can an infant do? What use can it be to an infant? In such a case, it is very true, it would be a difficult thing to discern any wisdom in the administration of an institution of any kind to an infant. And I remember once conversing with a Baptist upon infant baptism, who, among other things, observed what a silly thing it was to baptize an infant. As I perceived his views extended no further than helpless infancy, I asked him, whether, if he had seen it done, he would not have thought it a very silly thing to circumcise an infant? "That I should indeed," said he, "indeed I should;" these, as well as I can recollect, were his very words. But when, on the contrary, our views take in the grand design of engaging the attention the more fixedly to the rising race, all the supposed silliness vanishes away, and it appears a plan worthy the wisdom and kindness of God.

I was led more particularly to view the matter in this point of light, by considering that commission given to the apostles by the risen Saviour, respecting the Gentile nations, Matt. xxviii. 18, 19, 20. " All power is given unto me in heaven and in earth. Go ye therefore, and, *matheeteusate*, disciple all nations, baptizing them in the name of the Father, and of the Son, and of the Holy Ghost; *didaskontes*, teaching them to observe all things whatsoever I have commanded you, &c." Here we have the whole plan just as I have set it down in the case of circumcision: they are sent to make disciples (scholars;) for *discipulus* in Latin, and scholar in English, are just the same; they are to enter such as are made scholars by baptism; they are to instruct these scholars in the things of Christ, in order that they may observe them. Our blessed Lord, by making use of the words *matheeteusate*, make disciples, and *didaskontes*, teaching, carries our views immediately to *matheetai, discipuli*, scholars, and *didaskaloi, præceptores*, school-masters; and thus we are presented with a Christian school with scholars and masters.

According to this view of the subject, and to this our Lord's words naturally lead us, there appears not only a grandeur of design, but likewise an exact symmetry in the different dispensations of God—I mean that attention to the rising offspring, which had shown itself in a former dispensation, and, no doubt, in all. It is to be observed that our Lord uses a term, a school term, which will agree to an infant as well as an adult; for the word *matheetees*, a scholar, of which the word used by our Lord is the theme, does not necessarily intend previous learning nor present learning, but only learning in design. We call those scholars, who have done learning, and so we do those who are now at their studies, and so likewise those who have not yet begun to learn, provided they are entered for that purpose: so that the idea of learning does not necessarily annex itself to the term *matheetees*, scholar, any further than to denote a person who is entered into a school with a view to learn.

But here it may be asked, What propriety can there be, in calling a person a disciple or scholar, who is yet incapable of learning? I reply, he is properly so called, because he is entered with that design: *e. g.* Numbers iii. 28. "In the number of all the males, from a month old and upwards, were eight thousand and six hundred, keeping the charge of the sanctuary." Can any body tell me how a child of six weeks old could be a keeper of the charge of the sanctuary? Certainly he could no otherwise be called a keeper, but as one designed and appointed to that service. Just with the same propriety, an infant, who, by circumcision or baptism, was or is publicly entered into a religious school, may be called a disciple in a religious sense. And it is a very general opinion, that infants are actually so called in Acts xv. 10. "Why tempt ye God to put a yoke on the neck of the disciples?" That infants are called disciples will appear plain, if we ask, On whose neck was this yoke to have come? Every one knows, who knows the manner of Moses respecting circumcision, that it would have come on adults, but chiefly on infants; and then it is evident, that as part of those, on whom the yoke would have come, were infants, it is as evident, that those infants were called disciples: but whether this be so or not, the word made use of by our Lord will agree to infants as well as adults.

The apostles are to make disciples—that is all *matheeteusate* imports. But still the question is, How are they to make them? I answer, By teaching; for neither adult nor infant can be made a disciple without. And herein the Baptists are very right, and I agree with them, that adults and infants must be made disciples by teaching, or they will not be made so at all. But then how can an infant be made a disciple by teaching? I reply, not directly, but indirectly; that is, the parents, being won over by teaching to embrace the truth, they present their infants to the Christian school to be trained up in the same truth; and thus they become disciples: *e. g.* Joel is to sanctify a fast, and call a solemn assembly, to gather the people, elders, children, and those that suck the breasts. But how is he to assemble them? He is to blow a trumpet in Zion. But what does a sucking child know about the sound of a trumpet? I answer, he knows nothing at all about it. How then are sucking children to be brought together by the sound of a trumpet, seeing they know nothing of the trumpet or its sound? I reply

In the same way as infants are made disciples by teaching. But how is that? Every one knows how it is, who knows any thing; and this I have already explained. If the trumpet had not been sounded, the sucklings would not have been collected, and if men were not taught, infants would not become disciples: so then infants as well as men are made disciples by teaching, as elders and sucking children are brought to the fast by the sound of a trumpet.

Viewing baptism as introducing infants into a visible state of discipleship, we are to consider others as teachers and overlookers of these disciples; and then the usefulness of such an institution will display itself before us. We see an infant baptized. If our views terminate there, alas! what is it? Infant sprinkling only, the baptism of a baby. Things which are little in themselves, become great by their connexion with, and relation to, others. We see an infant baptized—What does it import? He is received into discipleship, *i. e.* to be a scholar in a Christian school. Now carry your views into the department of parents, pastors, deacons, and members; and listen to the silent language of this institution. "Parents, pastors, and people, pray for us; during our tender infancy, pray for us. And when matured by age, cause the doctrine which you profess, to drop upon us as the rain, to distil as dew, as the small rain upon the tender herb, and as showers upon the grass. Watch over us with united care, and bring us up in the nurture and admonition of the Lord." It is a dispensation grand and merciful, which is calculated more powerfully to turn the attention of men to the concerns of those who are rising into life, and posting into eternity.

There is one fault among others in the Baptist system, that it places the rising generation so entirely out of sight. I do not mean that the Baptists themselves do this; for their conduct in this respect is much better than their system; but their system places them out of sight. And in this, it differs from all the dispensations of God, of which we have any particular knowledge; which alone would lead to a presumption, that it is not of God.

To what I have said concerning the use of infant baptism, under the idea of an institution suited to draw the attention more powerfully to the immortal concerns of the rising generation, (and he must be very inattentive to human nature, who does not see a beauty and blessedness in such a contrivance;) there is no objection that can be brought by a Baptist, but may be retorted. He may say, Cannot all this be done without baptizing infants? Retort: cannot men be built up in faith and love, without either baptism or the Lord's supper?—Are not many baptized infants as destitute of real religion as others? Ret.—And are not many baptized adults, as destitute of religion as heathens? Are not many unbaptized infants brought up in Christian knowledge equally as well as the baptized ones? Ret.—And are not many, who have not been baptized in adult age, as gracious and holy as those who have? In this way every objection which can be brought may easily be retorted on the objector.

But the truth is, that the enjoyment of ordinances is to be considered only as a means of grace; they are well suited as ordinances to impress the mind; but then, it is very certain, they effect nothing, unless God is pleased to give the increase. The possession of the word of God, the enjoyment of preaching, baptism, the Lord's supper, are good things in themselves, though many are never the better for them; but we are to estimate these things not by the advantage which some receive, but by their own suitableness to promote, as means, some great ends.

When we consider infants under the notion of disciples, or scholars, the idea suggests to us a noble kind of discipline in the church of God. It suggests, that all those infants who were baptized, should be formed, as they become capable, into societies, for the purpose of Christian instruction; and so every church should have its school. That there should be in churches, not only *poimenes*, pastors, but *didaskaloi*, schoolmasters, Eph. iv. 11. That the minister, and other fit persons, should preside over these little disciples; and parents who bring their children to baptism, should consider themselves as bound in con science to see them forth-coming to this society at all appointed seasons. That all the members should watch over them, with respect to their morals, and likewise their Christian learning. In short, the whole should be a church business, regulated in the manner of doing according to the wisdom of each Christian society. For as the infant is received by the church as a disciple in its baptism, the church becomes bound to regard that infant as such; and to see that it is treated as a scholar of Christ. To all this, it is plain, the idea of discipleship leads; and in this view it becomes greatly important, as its tendency is to draw the cares and prayers of the whole Christian church towards the rising generation.

There are many special uses connected with this grand leading idea, which the limit of this essay will not permit me to mention. I cannot say how far the leading idea itself is attended to by those who adopt infant baptism; if it be not, it is so much the more to be lamented, that in this, as well as in other things, the spirit of an institution is not followed up to its proper scope. It is sufficient, notwithstanding, to my present purpose, in showing the usefulness of an ordinance, if there be a natural fitness, in the ordinance itself, to promote the great end I have mentioned. And as every system we embrace is likely to impress our minds according to its nature; that system must be eminently good and useful, which is calculated, most of all, to bring the rising generation, and their everlasting concerns to our mind; to hold them up perpetually before our eyes; and to fix them habitually upon our hearts.—All this the admission of infants by baptism to a state of discipleship in the church of God, is evidently calculated to do ; and herein I judge its main usefulness consists.

THE END.

www.ingramcontent.com/pod-product-compliance
Lightning Source LLC
Chambersburg PA
CBHW021013240426
43669CB00037B/945